Practical Computer Ethics

Duncan Langford

D1121182

McGRAW-HILL BOOK COMPANY
London · New York · St Louis · San Francisco · Auckland
Bogotá · Caracas · Lisbon · Madrid · Mexico · Milan
Montreal · New Delhi · Panama · Paris · San Juan
São Paulo · Singapore · Sydney · Tokyo · Toronto

Published by
McGraw-HILL Book Company Europe
Shoppenhangers Road, Maidenhead, Berkshire, SL6 2QL, England
Telephone 01628 23432
Fax 01628 770224

British Library Cataloguing in Publication Data
Langford, Duncan
Practical Computer Ethics
I. Title
174.9
ISBN 0-07-709012-8

Library of Congress Cataloging-in-Publication Data
Langford, Duncan
Practical computer ethics / Duncan Langford.
    p.   cm.
Includes bibliographical references and index.
ISBN 0-07-709012-8 (pbk.: acid-free paper)
1. Electronic data processing—Moral and ethical aspects.
I. Title.
QA76.9.M65L36   1995   95–2503
174'.90904—dc20   CIP

McGraw-Hill

A Division of The **McGraw-Hill** Companies

345 CUP 98

Typeset by Paston Press Ltd, Norfolk
Printed and bound in Great Britain at the University Press, Cambridge

Printed on permanent paper in compliance with ISO Standard 9706

To Gina and Maddy
the much loved women in my life

And what is good, Phaedrus,
And what is not good
Need we ask anyone to tell us these things?

Robert M. Pirsig
Zen and the Art of Motorcycle Maintenance

Contents

Acknowledgements

I am greatly indebted to all those individuals who have given me permission to use their experiences as the basis of illustrative examples. Their help was invaluable. (Most names and identifying details have, of course, been changed.)

Thanks, also, to the Open University for the material in Appendix A, and Ken Cambell, of Ontario's *eye* magazine, for the material in Appendix C; the Institution of Analysts and Programmers for the material in Appendix D, and to the British Computer Society (BCS) and Association for Computing Machinery (ACM) for permission to reproduce their Codes of Conduct as Appendix E. The Rand Corporation, of Santa Monica, California, was good enough to allow an extract from its document 'Toward an Ethics and Etiquette for Electronic Mail', which forms the basis of the email guidelines suggested in Chapter 9.

My colleagues in the Computing Laboratory of the University of Kent were patient and supportive. The UKC Systems Group, especially Godfrey Paul, were particularly helpful in answering technical queries concerning the practical management of computer systems.

Chapter 7 is largely based, with his kind permission, upon my contribution to Colin Myers' *Professional Awareness in Software Engineering*, McGraw-Hill, London, 1995.

Introduction

What's this book about?

Practical Computer Ethics is emphatically not an ethics text for ethicists. This introduction explains what it is.

I must make it clear immediately that this book is not a work of theoretical analysis and discussion. *Practical Computer Ethics* is not for academic philosophers.

However, if you are, or you intend to become, a practising computer scientist; or you work with computers, or are responsible for computer systems – this book is directed specifically at you.

There is a widely felt and growing need for those working with computers, and especially computing students, to have an understanding and appreciation of ethics. This view is held by many university computing courses, and is supported enthusiastically by the British Computer Society, among others. Unfortunately, many existing ethical texts are written either from a formal standpoint; are primarily concerned with computer crime issues; or have an American focus. Ethics material is often also seen as dull and hard to read – which is a fault I have tried to avoid.

The purpose of this book is to explain in plain language the background to the development of a personal ethical code, and give consideration to the potentially vast range of ethical issues within computing. It helps to identify specific areas within computing practice where ethical problems are likely, and suggests ways in which issues may be resolved. It also describes the principal UK legislation, and professional codes of conduct.

This book is built on the practical lessons I have gained from teaching ethics to computer scientists, and particularly from talking and exchanging email with many people who have experienced ethical problems when working with computer systems. Using this material freely, I have always tried to illustrate points with examples of actual ethical issues experienced by real people – although, naturally, the identifying details of cases have been changed.

Practical Computer Ethics deals directly with practical ethical problems commonly involved in designing, developing and supporting computer systems and applications, and is intended specifically for computer scientists working in the 'real world'.

Study questions

Each chapter ends with a list of questions, intended for discussion in class or seminar – or, of course, by individuals.

However, do not assume that there is an appropriate, approved solution to any of these questions. As will become clear, there are very few clear cut 'right' and 'wrong' answers in the field of computer ethics.

1

Why *should* hard-nosed computer professionals be concerned with a wimpy subject like Ethics?

This chapter considers why even busy computer scientists need to spend time thinking about ethical issues.

Is there a distinct difference between people working in a scientific field, and those concerned with 'Arts' subjects? Most of us are probably aware of anecdotal evidence suggesting that this is so. Typically, scientists are thought to see themselves as logical beings, concerned solely with facts. However, to those working in other fields, scientists concentrating on the issue at hand may appear unwilling – or unable – to appreciate wider issues.

Certainly, an objective, quantifying approach is common to most science teaching, forming a 'scientific' method understood and accepted as the way things are done. When teaching ethics, I have sometimes found computer scientists showing feelings almost of distaste when confronted by a topic that clearly did not fall neatly into the familiar and comfortable pattern of a science subject.

'What', one said, in a burst of honesty, 'can this wimpy subject have to do with me? I'm a *scientist.*' It was easy to tell, just by the tone of voice, his pride in that title. For years he had been certain what it meant: choices had been made before A levels, and he did not intend to allow contamination now by some ill-defined Arts subject. 'Science' was solid, dealt in real things – and, as a bonus, was probably macho, too. Arts subjects, in contrast, were vague, hard to define, and concerned themselves too much with intangibles.

This view is not at all unusual[1] – you may hold it yourself. Even a polite computer scientist's description of a non-science subject probably involves words like 'woolly'. Our training and experience as scientists have shown us that science is important – and science is seldom woolly? If this perception is true, it would obviously be unreasonable to expect busy professionals to believe there is much to be gained from time spent on such a topic. Accepting a non-science subject as professionally important may not be easy.

This chapter looks briefly at possible reasons for such a state of affairs, before attempting to extract from what admittedly appears to be a very woolly subject – ethics – some essential points which make it a vital issue for computer scientists.

Scientists are different

Let us look at this issue more closely, and try to determine what the debate is really about.

People do not start out qualified. Although there may of course be natural skills, no one is born a scientist, or indeed born any sort of specialist. Throughout childhood and adolescence, the knowledge which forms an adult is informally acquired and formally taught. It is reasonable to assume that specialists develop their attitudes and views as a result of their formal training; so are scientists – particularly computer scientists – perhaps trained in a different manner from 'Arts' students?

It would undoubtedly be wrong to accept unquestioningly the views of a friend with a degree in American Literature: she considers all science subject teaching as essentially involving presentation of numerous facts by the teacher and assimilation of them by the student. However, we can perhaps admit that, although comprehension and understanding are clearly fundamental, an essential part of most science teaching lies in making students aware of a clearly defined body of knowledge that is not *itself* susceptible to individual opinion. Teaching how to develop complex database queries, for instance, must be founded on understanding and appropriate use of suitable procedures. A personal wish to find individual new methods for each transaction is not appropriate.

In contrast, students of American Literature will be positively encouraged to develop individual views of their subject. Such views would of course be based on established research, but any student who proved incapable of demonstrating an independent opinion would not do well. Unlike our unfortunate student of computer science, a literature student is expected to criticize established belief.

This is very much a simplification, but the basic position is surely clear – scientists are trained to understand and assimilate large quantities of established facts. Disciplines other than science may set aside space to encourage development of individual views. However, without strong incentives, under the timetable pressures of most computer science courses this aspect of education is unlikely to gain much of a following.

Why does this matter?

Fact-based training is reinforced by practical experience. A computer science (CS) student – or a CS professional – is continually presented with statements that do not permit any individual colouration: 'This instruction won't compile'; 'C++ inheritance takes this form'; and so on. Such statements may or may not be *accepted*, but their *truth* is unquestioned.

Such a working environment confirms and consolidates the experiences of scientific training. It also encourages a view that the wider world is likely to operate in a similar way: that most problems may be precisely defined, and issues beyond those immediately related to the current problem are not relevant. Importantly, it also suggests there will probably be an answer to most questions, and that someone in authority – a lecturer, manager or team leader – will generally be able to provide it.

A simple example illustrates this point.

John worked in the computing department of a mail order company. His team had been given the task of automating a regular mailshot to customers – the idea was to remind them about the state of their account, notify them of interesting new items and so on. Customers had a local agent, who was originally sent copies of each letter. John was asked to modify the program so that, instead of multiple copies, the local agent received a single letter containing details of the amount owed by each of that agent's customers. A junior manager suggested simplifying things further, so the same letter went to local agent and local customers alike. John programmed the changes without worrying about their results. As a direct consequence, personal details of an individual's debts were sent to all other customers in their area.

In this case, the danger was identified before the letters were actually posted – but John, satisfied with solving a tricky problem, remained unaware of any responsibility, and was very surprised at the serious view taken of his work.

In order to find a solution, it is clearly necessary to focus precisely on a problem; but if this focusing excludes broader issues – and especially if the scientist trusts those in authority to take care of such things – then there may well be difficulties. In the case of a computer scientist, whose work can have wide-ranging effects, these difficulties could be extensive.

What can be done?

The situation is, of course, not a new one. In the UK, as in most technologically advanced countries, there are laws governing the use of computers, and punishing their misuse. Such laws (described in more detail in Chapter 6) have perhaps been influenced more by public pressure than the desire of computer scientists to be appropriately regulated. While providing some restrictions, laws may leave uncovered much which is potentially damaging.

Development of suitable statutes is clearly necessary; but, even if comprehensive laws existed, would it be reasonable to argue that every strictly legal action must always be appropriate?

To assist the concerned specialist in deciding upon appropriate professional conduct there is of course 'professional' help, described more fully in Chapter 7. Most, if not all, sciences have their own professional society, and such bodies – for computer scientists in the UK, the British Computer Society, or BCS – provide guidelines and codes of practice on professional issues. Such documents are undoubtedly valuable; but however well written and researched they may be, professional codes cannot cover every situation a member may encounter, or always provide sufficient personal support.

I believe the only truly satisfactory answer is for all professional computer scientists to develop an awareness of their own, individual, values. While such values should of course be influenced by knowledge of the law, professional codes and experience, they must be founded upon a bedrock of personal beliefs.

Once established, codes of personal values may be applied to any uncertainty, personal or professional. Individual awareness of such a set of personal values, or 'ethics', is not just convenient – for scientists in today's complex society it is becoming increasingly essential.

Ethics?

This section deals very briefly with the general background to ethical studies. If you are not interested in how computer ethics relates to the study of philosophy, you may jump to the next section.

The ancient Greeks probably issued the first prospectus, and there have been many interested philosophers since. Philosophy, as a subject, has clearly been around for some time. 'Philosophy' itself is really an umbrella term, which covers several interrelated subjects – metaphysics, which studies reality, is probably the best known. That branch of philosophy which deals with human conduct and character is known as 'moral' philosophy, or ethics.

Practical ethics – the subject of this book – is that component of ethics which deals with personal uncertainties and conflicts of opinion: 'What choice should I take?', 'Is this action unfair?', and so on. It is of course possible to step further back, and ask wider questions which attempt to analyse more general standards: 'If this action is said to be right, what does "right" really mean?' and other such queries. This larger scale analysis is known as theoretical ethics.

The study of what moral beliefs are actually held by a society is called 'descriptive' ethics, and could claim to be a branch of sociology. In contrast, the prescription of authoritative standards based upon accepted norms within a society is known as 'normative' ethics, or sometimes 'philosophical' ethics.

These terms may well be confusing. Fortunately, for our purposes it is not necessary to learn them. Although a fascinating study, a description of the history and development of moral philosophy, or ethics, lies outside the scope of this book. There is, however, a wide range of philosophical writing, and those interested in finding out more should study the Bibliography.

Ethics for scientists?

Despite the long history of ethics, or perhaps because of it, there are no universally accepted sets of moral rules for a scientist to study. The subject is not 'scientific', and this lack of a traditional scientific base may have obscured the fact that possessing a concept of ethics could be of considerable help to scientists.

The act of living in the world brings responsibilities – and there are factors which, like it or not, must be considered by everyone. If, for example, individuals are unaware of the consequences of their actions, their responsibility does not vanish. If I did not actually realize that pulling out this plug to hook up my computer disconnected a life-support system, would that satisfy the coroner?

It is not enough, morally or legally, to be content to follow instructions, either. Trust in authority is obviously important, but can be taken to extremes – 'I was only obeying orders' is not so different from a belief that 'they' must always have good, if sometimes obscure, reasons. Delegation of ethical responsibility in this way is seldom appropriate.

Individuals have a responsibility to discover the consequences of their actions, and to take responsibility for themselves. Although it may at first appear so, this is emphatically not a recipe for 'goodness'. When all the facts are known to you, the decision to be taken is the one that is ethically appropriate *for you*. An example may make this clearer:

> Wendy is a systems analyst. Her company has been asked to report on a proposal to monitor employees of a multinational bank by intercepting data flowing through company-owned computer systems.
>
> The proposal is legal, but Wendy is worried. She therefore obtains more details, and discovers the interception is to be kept secret: the bank's intention is to provide support for a plan to close down their UK operation.

Could a knowledge of ethics help Wendy?

The conventional solution to this example is predictably obvious – Wendy should decide against participating in a clandestine monitoring operation. Certainly, most of us might find the ethics of such a task dubious. However, I contend the issue is, rather, whether *Wendy* finds the job unethical. That decision is for her to make. If, after thinking through all the implications, she decides to go ahead, then that – for her – is the appropriate decision.

The vitally important part of this process lies in gathering facts and 'thinking them through'. A decision based on poor data, for instance, or one that relied solely on obedience to instructions, would not be justified. Ethics consequently does not define and then impose a defined set of values, and demand that those approved values must always be followed slavishly by everyone.

What, then, *does* an appreciation of ethics do? It encourages individuals to think through their attitudes and beliefs, and thus be able to decide in advance what they believe is appropriate behaviour for *them*. It is important, once this is decided, that individuals should then be prepared to accept full responsibility for their actions.

What is relevant for me?

What can an appreciation of ethics give to a computer professional? There are numerous reasons, which naturally vary in significance from individual to individual; many are described in the following chapters.

Three incentives that may be particularly important to you are :

- Trust: an individual known to operate under a consistent code of personal ethics is one who can be relied upon.
- Security: being aware of the implications of your actions guards against unexpected outcomes.
- Comfort: this is admittedly subjective; but peace of mind is probably the most important benefit of all.

Who would wish to live in a society where computer systems are designed without reference to ethics – or personally choose to work with constantly changing ethical standards?

I believe all computer scientists would gain from consideration of ethics; despite its woolly image, the subject is actually fiercely relevant.

Conclusions

Ethics allows – *insists* upon – introduction of individual human opinions and beliefs into areas previously thought to be exclusively 'business' or 'scientific'. It encourages consideration of the wider issues involved in professional judgements, and provides support for individuals who may find the monolithic pressures of a competitive, market economy driven society otherwise overwhelming.

Lacking clear global definitions and an accepted rule set, ethics is not an obvious subject for scientific attention; but thinking about ethics nevertheless makes personal and professional sense.

Questions

1. What do you understand by 'ethics'? Write down three or four words which you feel appropriately describe the subject, and, if possible, compare them with the views of others.

    Save these notes; they will be needed later.
2. Would you describe yourself as a 'scientist'? What characteristics do you feel scientists possess, that distinguish them from other professionals?
3. Can you think of any reasons why *you* should act ethically?
4. Can you think of any reasons why *others* should act ethically?
5. Are there any differences between your answers to the two previous questions? Why might this be?

Note

[1] See, for example, 'There's More to Science and Skills Shortages than Demography and Economics: attitudes to science and technology degrees and careers', Alison Fuller, *Studies in Higher Education*, **16**(3) 1991, pp. 333–41.

2

Developing personal concepts

This chapter looks at where personal views actually come from, and on what they are based.

Influences on individuals may arrive from unexpected directions. What may seem at first to be a 'personal' view or opinion may turn out to be the reflection of something very different. How may influences be distinguished?

A useful first point to establish is that personal codes of conduct, whether they are 'ethical' ones or not, are by no means new. Even if you are not aware of it – and many people are not – you probably already possess a set of controlling opinions, together with their related internal rules. Such rules are probably very similar in structure, if not in content, to a formal ethical code, and form a set of beliefs of which you may well be unconscious.

Why is the question of 'unconscious beliefs' important? It is important because what people believe affects the way they live. This means that, whether you may be conscious of them or not, such hidden opinions may already exert control over your life.

One aim of this book is to make you aware of how values are acquired, what may influence the process, and how you can consciously affect it. This is relevant, because it is only when you understand where personal views come from that you may be sure of the views you hold, and can introduce appropriate ethical beliefs. You can then begin to gain conscious control over the relationship between what you may believe and what you actually do.

Generally, of course, life is not lived out as a philosophy text. Instead of following the popular image of philosophers, and spending most of our time thinking deeply about what we believe, we are all used to letting our lives develop 'naturally', and accepting whatever our beliefs may be without question. Of course, once the issue is raised, we can naturally agree that we do hold individual beliefs and ideas. Surely they are unique, original and *ours*, rather than accepted, imported or recycled from other people?

If we start to wonder about what we believe, and where our ideas came from, the immediate and obvious conclusion is indeed that our opinions are original, and come from within us. This explanation may certainly at first seem to be correct; but can it really be true? It is possibly a rather unsettling thought, to consider that this may not be so. Surely we believe what we do believe because our views are ours, and therefore automatically right; and *not* because a television advertisement influenced us, or we were told what to think by an employer?

However, this reassuring view of things is unfortunately false. No one is born with a fixed set of values – what we believe now is the end result of life experiences, gained during our upbringing, through the influences of care-givers and school, and, later on, in the experiences of adult life.

Once we begin to think about them, some of these influences may be obvious, while others are perhaps rather more difficult to identify.

> Jakob was a student, working in the office of a software engineering company as a summer project. He spent much time chatting to the team leader, who enjoyed passing on his experiences and talking about bending rules on his 'journey to the top'. Jakob was impressed.
>
> Back in class, after returning to college, Jakob argued for rule breaking. In the argument that followed, several students challenged Jakob's views. Class discussion helped him to realize where 'his' views had come from. Many of the edited events he had heard on his placement had given Jakob a distorted view of founding a successful career. Knowledge of this encouraged him to look for another side.

This illustration is not intended to suggest that Jakob's original view – rule breaking is OK – was 'right' or 'wrong'. What is important is that Jakob's eventual views were based on an understanding of the whole picture, rather than one part of it. If, after considering all the issues, he decided in favour of a code which allowed such behaviour, it might still qualify as 'ethical'.

The important point is to be aware of the source of your views, in order to be sure, *before* finally adopting them, that opinions are genuinely yours.

> Jenny works as a data entry clerk for a large office in London; her job involves typing information into a terminal. Jenny makes no attempt to think about what she is typing, far less checking to confirm that it is ethical, or even legal.
>   When interviewed, she explained she knew it was all right; monitoring the data was her employer's responsibility.

In this case it may well have been 'all right'; but it is not hard to think what an unscrupulous employer might consider to be appropriate material. Jenny's action in leaving all the worrying to her employer is certainly quite understandable. However, trusting your employer to continually do the right thing may not always be wise; and it certainly makes a very poor defence, should things go wrong. Of course not all cases are as straightforward as Jenny's – but she certainly is not alone in refusing to think about what she was doing because it was someone else's responsibility.

> Hassan was a newly appointed data processing manager within a small UK manufacturing company. While familiarizing himself with the accounting systems, he became aware that his predecessor had arranged to disguise payments made by a senior sales manager, apparently to secure contracts. At first Hassan was assured this was 'normal business practice', but he was unconvinced. The crunch came when he was instructed by the Sales Director to leave the existing procedures in place, and to stop concerning himself with the matter. Although it might have seemed easy to turn a blind eye, Hassan felt unable to do so, and resigned. (He made no explanation, and gained a good reference; it is unclear whether the company ever connected his resignation with the issue.)

I suggested in the previous chapter that it was appropriate for computer scientists to acquire a concept of ethics. The concept, once understood, could be used by an individual to develop and maintain an internal view of what was right and appropriate for them. The next section explores this background, and looks at the question in a little more detail.

Where do personal values come from?

Jenny did not claim to have any relevant views, but was this true? She certainly had a belief that her employer was to be trusted, and, therefore, that any work she was given was so likely to be ethically appropriate that no further checking by her was necessary. In short, Jenny did hold a relevant view – a very simple one. She equated the ethical standards of her employer with her own. Therefore, what was appropriate for Jenny's employer must, automatically, be appropriate for her.

This view may, of course, sometimes be correct, but should be accepted only after the employees concerned have themselves fully evaluated the situation. Such evaluation is essential – the views of employer and employee seldom exactly coincide, and even good employers sometimes take an understandably biased view. 'What's good for General Motors is good for the country', as GM President Charles Wilson memorably asserted at his 1953 Senate confirmation hearing as US Secretary of Defense.

> Lee and Brian were programmers, in the same team. Lee had worked there for a year; Brian had just joined. Brian, stuck on a tricky bit of coding, asked Lee for help. Lee advised him to quietly 'lift' specialist code from another project, already charged to a different customer. 'Pinch some code. Everybody does it.'

Such an action is potentially illegal, and certainly ethically dubious. Taking someone else's code, and pretending that it is yours – where did Lee get his values? They probably came from the same place that Brian is about to learn his – from the common practice of their workplace. Of course, to us, looking at Brian's experience as example, the position is clearer than it was to him. From a distance, it is much easier to see that, because values are common in a particular site, they are not necessarily equally valued everywhere.

> Jerry stole computer equipment from his college, the latest of a number of offences of theft. Both Jerry's parents, and two of his siblings, had theft convictions going back many years.

Without excusing his actions, it is very likely that Jerry's view of the ethics of stealing computer equipment was influenced by the opinions of his family. In just the same way, Lee's attitude to 'pinching' code was influenced by his workplace.

A person's views may therefore be affected by their family and workplace, but are there other areas of influence? Clearly, there are, and in fact the number of such possible pressures is potentially huge. Human interaction is recursive – every aspect of the way in which individuals react with those around them in turn colours the way they perceive the world, and so modifies their interaction with it.

If we view the individual as being at the centre of surrounding influences, it is possible to display some of these pressures in diagrammatic form (Figure 2.1).

The individual, at the centre of the figure, is surrounded by his or her closest influences – those of family and friends, representing social life, and working colleagues, representing the work environment. A division between the 'work' and 'home' influences makes for a clearer figure, although of course working colleagues often share social activities. In practice the two areas frequently blend.

The closer the source of influence, the greater its effect on a person is likely to be. This is best understood with a simple inverse example. Consider a person who constantly plays their favourite compact disc (CD) at high volume. Should they chance to live next door, the CD would undoubtedly become a nuisance to you fairly quickly, however much you

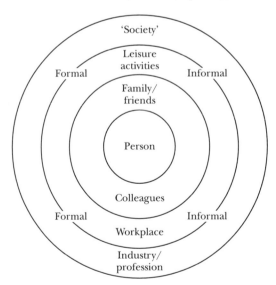

Figure 2.1.   Influences on an individual

may have initially liked it. However, if, instead, it was played at the other end of the road, you might hear only distant snatches of the tune, and your original opinion of it would remain unaffected.

A similar process is true of personal opinions, and the various formal and informal rules which govern both work and leisure.

Conclusions

This chapter has discussed how what you may believe to be your 'personal' views may actually reflect the convictions of those around you, rather than your own uncoloured opinions. The views of employer or colleagues, family and friends, however satisfactory to them, and however potentially valid to you, must be assessed and carefully considered before being incorporated into your own beliefs.

To accept unquestioningly the opinions of others can never allow construction of a valid set of personal ethical values. It is essential to spend time analysing and identifying what you *are* confident are your genuine personal beliefs, and, in particular, to distinguish them from what might prove to be merely responses to external manipulation and pressure. It is only on a core of such 'authentic' beliefs that an individual set of ethical values may be built.

Questions

1. Can you identify any 'core' beliefs? Where do you feel your beliefs may have come from?
2. Can you identify any area where the attitudes of your colleagues or classmates have influenced what you believe, or perhaps what you did?
3. What distinguishes your views from those of the people with whom you live and work?
4. Is it possible to identify an external pressure on you which had an effect on what you believe?

3

Identifying ethical problems

Exactly what is an 'ethical' problem in computing? How may such problems be identified? After looking briefly at the background to ethical discussions, this chapter examines some typical problems in the field of computing, and discusses what they might involve. Possible resolutions are covered in the next chapter.

General discussion of 'ethical problems' has tended to be of somewhat traditional form, often using fairly unlikely examples. For instance, a typical example of the ethical problems you may have discussed at school might be the classic – 'In a burning house, you can save either a cat or a masterpiece by Rembrandt; which do you choose?' The illustration is intended to bring out the value of 'art' in comparison with 'life'.

Exactly what consideration of this case actually provides is unclear. Few of us possess masterpieces by Rembrandt, and although rather more may own cats, it is surely an unusually lazy animal which wishes to be carried from a burning building.

If you have not experienced the Rembrandt fire, you may have come across another ethics classic – 'If, by pressing a button, you could simultaneously gain a million pounds, but also cause the death of an anonymous unknown on the other side of the world, would you do so?'

Think, the argument runs, of what could be done with the million pounds – the medical research, the lives that could be saved. Wait – runs the counter argument – that anonymous person may be or become another Mozart, or a Shakespeare. Or perhaps another Hitler, rejoins the counter argument – and so the whole artificial case creaks round and round. Whatever may be learned from such time-honoured examples, it is unlikely to be related to your daily routines or situation.

Because it is all too easy to criticize such cases, I'd better make it clear that by doing so I do not intend to play down the importance of considering and discussing ethical issues and examples. Discussion should always be encouraged. For this reason, if we discard these veteran examples, it should be to exchange them for more suitable replacements.

A key theme of this book is the belief that necessarily abstract discussions on 'ethics' should have maximum weight, and, particularly, should bring home the genuine relevance of ethics to individuals. Such discussions should therefore not be based on concocted and impossible scenarios, but on examples close to real life. Further: the examples used should not only come from life, but should feature practical issues which are likely to be faced by those involved in the discussion.

For example, few individuals actually have to decide about protecting their Rembrandt, but everyone using a computer is concerned over protecting their files. While no one actually agonizes over an abstract reward at the expense of an abstract death, software engineers certainly agonize over reconciling the implementation of a system with the demands and budget of the client.

For these reasons, examples in this chapter (and in this book) are drawn from life,[1] and are intended to reflect actual problems that may be experienced by those working with the field of computing. Happily, no one is likely to be unfortunate enough to experience them all, but most people who have spent time in the computing industry will certainly recognize at least some of these issues.

Defining problems

As discussed earlier, an individual's underlying ethical philosophy is applicable to all aspects of that person's life, including, of course, computing. To this extent, there can consequently be no allocation of computing issues for judgement against some unique 'ethics of computing', because such a thing does not and cannot exist. Any professional code of conduct must be founded upon generally accepted standards of conduct and behaviour, and, because it reflects and supports such standards, it cannot replace them. The best way to understand why an all-embracing 'ethics of computing' or indeed an 'ethics of anything' is impossible, is by looking at the alternative.

Should such a uniquely specialized code be possible, each profession and discipline would become able to develop and impose an exclusive definition of what was and was not appropriate conduct. A huge variety of such different 'codes' from special interest groups would consequently struggle against each other, with no external measure by which they could be evaluated. If there were no agreed and generally accepted codes of behaviour, by which of the many different and conflicting rules could people then be judged?

In 12th century England, the clergy lived under their own code of behaviour and law. Even when a priest committed a secular crime, he was judged by a religious court – there was, literally, one law for the clergy and one for everyone else. The results of the split were certainly appreciated by the church, but bitterly resented by all others, from the king downward. Even then, though, an underlying view of what was ethical behaviour was shared between priest and lay people. If they disagreed over who should decide an appropriate punishment, there was generally agreement over what was considered right and wrong.

However, consider what would happen if every special interest group were able to define and hold its own, specialist, standards. Then, even though a member of one group behaved 'ethically' by maintaining its unique standards, such a person might easily be seen by members of other groups, with conflicting standards, as 'unethical'. Which standards and criteria could then be used to define a group? If a person belonged to more than one group, which alternative standards should be followed? Variable ones, to reflect the altered roles an individual may take at different social and work groupings throughout the day? The resultant confusion would clearly be enormous; the impossibility of living by such a scheme is plain. Dynamic, transferable sets of rules are no substitute for a consistent individual ethical code.

Once someone's general standards of ethical behaviour have been established, these personal standards should therefore be applied to every circumstance, whether this relates to the work of a specialist group or the business of everyday living. It is only when circumstances are new or unusual, or perhaps radically changed, that there may be room for considering additional 'special' ethical codes, but they should normally supplement, rather than replace, the existing accepted codes of behaviour.

Where special professional codes are of value is in defining particular areas of potential difficulty and providing examples of appropriate conduct. As is discussed in detail in Chapter 7, because a professional code is built upon collective experiences, it brings a much fuller and more focused approach to professional work. Collectively, members possess wider experience. No individuals in their professional lives will experience all aspects of such a code, but most will see some part of it and benefit from the combined knowledge of their colleagues in applying agreed standards to wider professional experience.

Even when there is a case for the creation of 'special' ethical codes, then, these should be considered alongside existing personal ethical standards. Something which is normally considered unethical does not magically become perfectly acceptable just because it is considered from a specialist viewpoint.

> Kurt was working on the development of a new software package. A colleague had left for the day, but Kurt wanted to refer to some printed notes she had left in a locked desk drawer.
>
> Most people would accept that it would not be appropriate to break open the desk in order to get the notes. What, however, if Kurt had the ability to hack into a computer system, and access the original file which generated the printed notes? Is breaking into someone's electronic office comparable to breaking into a physical one?

In this case, accepting a fundamental right to privacy would mean Kurt should leave both desk and directory strictly alone. Using a computer does not convey any special right to ignore normal standards of behaviour. As this example illustrates, we should always start by applying 'general' standards of ethical behaviour to a situation, and certainly do so before considering whether the current circumstances may merit looking at things from a different viewpoint.

Once this important issue is clear, we can move on to accept that there undoubtedly are general issues which gain particular prominence when examined from a computing perspective. As discussed below, there will of course also be new problems, related to technical developments, for which traditional responses may not be appropriate.

In addition to the ethical problems experienced by any modern business, the computing profession is faced by both old problems in a new context and by entirely new problems brought about by a very different working environment. Consequently, problems involving computer ethics may be divided into those which are long established and a much smaller number of new issues which are unique to the computing sector.

In the first group of problems might be a computing consultant who uses his job to steal software and equipment; or who, in order to land a contract, pretends to possess knowledge he does not actually have.

The first case is obviously illegal as well as unethical; the other clearly unethical, but arguably not illegal. Of course, although these are illustrations which involve computers, with only very minor changes both examples could readily be adapted to other areas of business. Proper analysis of such problems would clearly permit responses developed elsewhere to be appropriately applied within the field of computing.

A second, much smaller group, of 'computer-specific' problems, consists of issues which are unique within the computing industry. This second set of problems consists of issues which did not exist in advance of the available technology. Unfortunately, this group is much less easy to define. An example might be an employer's ability to use 'smart' ID badges to generate data for the analysis of employee behaviour.

It is certain that the advent of computers, their wholesale replacement of staff, and, particularly, their associated abilities to store and rapidly search vast ranges of data, has brought inevitable changes to working practices and expectations. Indeed, computing brings a new set of problems to today's business managers, systems designers and software engineers – problems qualitatively very different from those faced by the filing card generation.

As well as awareness of these existing issues, it is also necessary to remember that use of computers additionally presents *dynamic* problems – what was technically impossible yesterday becomes feasible today, and may well be common practice tomorrow.

For example, development of specifically targeted mailshots is a familiar business technique. However, if such targets are selected following computerized analysis of spending patterns, based perhaps on credit card payments at supermarket tills, the resultant shift in emphasis may well need examination.

It is important to appreciate that the driving force of developing technology lies behind many decisions taken in the computing industry. Examples abound where technological implementation preceded discussion, if indeed discussion took place at all; and it is easy to see how this can happen. Once introduced, such new developments rapidly become entrenched, while later technical modification based on non-technical issues presents obvious and often insurmountable difficulties.

This central point, that *development of technology can easily outpace ethical development*, needs to be kept constantly in mind when issues involving ethics and computing are discussed. For this reason alone, it is essential for ethical issues to be considered as part of the normal design cycle, and not as an extra to be added late in software or product development.

When viewing the rapid pace of technical development and the way in which new technological measures are introduced, there is a strong case to be made for the establishment of local 'ethics committees' in spheres where computer research takes place. Such committees, composed of informed and qualified professionals, would automatically vet proposals for grants and research, based on consideration of ethical implications. In many ways this approach could usefully copy the existing medical ethics committees of teaching hospitals and universities. Just as research into new treatments, or novel operating methods, must be 'vetted' by the appropriate medical committee before they can be introduced, so a course of computing research or novel product development would be examined and vetted for wider ethical implications.

So far this chapter has made it clear that general ethical issues are still relevant within the field of computing, and suggested that there are two possible divisions which may be made when considering computer-related ethical issues. The first includes problems which the computing profession has in common with others, and here lessons from non-computing experiences (such as those relating to business ethics), may be usefully applied. The second contains issues unique to computing. It is principally with the 'computer-specific' issues raised by analysis of the second group that we are concerned. Consideration of 'computer' ethics can therefore begin with a flying start, by appropriately transferring successful lessons taken from other contexts.

Identifying ethical questions

While developing some ways in which we might categorize our task, I have so far talked in general terms about ethical issues and questions, but have not yet established just what computer scientists might consider these to be. This section looks more closely at identification of 'ethical' issues.

What *is not* an ethical issue?

First, it is probably useful to clarify what is not an ethical issue. Ethics is concerned with an individual's beliefs, and is therefore hard to define globally, but it is still possible to make some general points. A good rule of thumb is that an ethical question is one which addresses beliefs, rather than convenience. For example, not wanting to work late because an employer is forcing regular unpaid work may be an ethical problem; refusing a special request to work late through fear of missing your favourite television soap may not. Because ethics is founded on belief, not opinion,[2] individual views about ethical issues tend to be deeply held. It is also unlikely that ethical beliefs change frequently. If an action is appropriate on Monday, it is still likely to be appropriate on Tuesday – unless, of course, new information comes to light.

> Harold worked for a design company as a systems analyst, and was offered a transfer to another team. The work had a military connection, and Harold claimed it was unethical. Offered more money, he accepted the move.

Although Harold claimed to be concerned over an ethical issue, only he knows whether he was, perhaps, more concerned with bargaining counters. It is more acceptable to be viewed as ethical, than greedy.

In summary, an issue is less likely to be an ethical one if the individual views which define it are:

- Primarily concerned with convenience
- Founded on opinions, not beliefs
- Casually modified, or frequently changed

As they are founded upon individual beliefs, there must inevitably be a large grey area around a wider definition of ethical issues. As always, the individual must take personal responsibility for drawing an appropriate line.

So what is an ethical question?

Life presents us with a continual series of questions, together with a need for constant decisions. It is only because we are so used to this pattern that we are not immediately aware of it – for most questions, our day-to-day decision-making process is largely run on 'autopilot' (Figure 3.1). What questions does it decide? Not necessarily always major ones. Which product do we buy in a supermarket, which team to support, what television programme to watch – most people's lives are full of apparently simple choices. Ethics may be involved, of course. For example, some supermarket products may be tested on animals, and, although perfectly

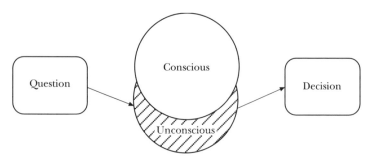

Figure 3.1   How our 'decision auto pilot' works.

adequate in themselves, may for that reason alone be left on the shelf. The 'image' of a particular sports team may present a stereotype of behaviour which is not acceptable to us – and so on.

Throughout childhood and adolescence we develop a view of what is right for us, and, whether we *consciously* apply it or not, this view influences our behaviour. (Where these views might come from is discussed in Chapter 2.)

In working life, the same rules apply. Whatever the level of our jobs, the constant demand for us to field questions and take decisions continues; the nature of the questions may grow more complex with a more responsible positions, but even a task of low status contains such demands.

Almost always, an individual will apply the lessons of everyday living to these problems, and field such questions without consciously thinking them through. This is because there is normally little to be gained by submitting every query and decision to a full analysis. There simply is not sufficient time to allow detailed examination of every issue – and it would be absurd to suggest otherwise. Unless the issue to be decided is very clearly a major one, or we are asked to take special steps, then reliance on our autopilot is understandable.

However, if reliance on an autopilot is necessary, it is clearly vital that we have programmed it correctly, and that we also have some mechanism for deciding when its use is inappropriate. Applying standard data to a non-standard situation is not recommended, even for the most advanced autopilot.

There are, then, two issues to decide. The first is the basic programming for our autopilot – what our essential beliefs are, and how we would want to interpret them. Once this has been established, we can safely leave the autopilot to handle everyday matters, allowing us to concentrate our energies and analysis on the inevitable special cases which it cannot handle. However, if we intend there to be special handling of some issues, it is obviously essential to determine in advance what these will be.

The second issue is therefore to decide definition criteria – what exactly will make a 'special' case? Possible factors are discussed below.

Preliminary analysis

Once the two points – basic beliefs, and the definitions of a special case – are established, they allow a new stage to be introduced into decision-making. Before any question is addressed, it is 'filtered', by being given a brief preliminary analysis. This first examination is just sufficient to determine whether the issue is one needing conscious decision or whether it may be processed automatically; that is, without the person concerned consciously analysing the details of that specific issue. At first, after this new stage is introduced, the individual will be aware that preliminary analysis is taking place. After the action becomes familiar, though, it will become less obtrusive – and will finally become virtually invisible. The huge mass of everyday questions will continue to pass, but, if balancing the issue against personal beliefs brings about a mismatch, conscious deliberation will automatically be called for. Simply, such an issue will fail to pass the 'filter' and will therefore be presented for conscious deliberation.

Incidentally, the filter may also be deliberately administered – 'does this issue raise any questions?', or may operate without the individual actually being aware of the process – 'this feels wrong'.

The original autopilot model must consequently be modified to reflect the addition of a new stage (Figure 3.2). Questions continue, but the addition of a filter now automatically presents some questions for conscious decision, while everything else is handled as before.

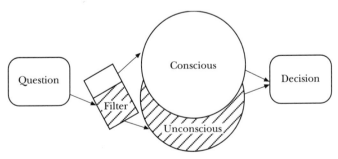

Figure 3.2 Adding a filter to the 'auto pilot'

Where do criteria come from?

I have said earlier that it is essential to start consideration of ethical issues within computing by first applying knowledge and experience from outside fields. This is clearly the primary source of criteria to be used by the 'filter'. Previous experience is also important in making both conscious and unconscious decisions. As discussed in Chapter 2, such knowledge comes from the influences and experiences of, among others, home and school, workplace and social life. More structured influences may come from consideration of the views of a professional organization or knowledge of the law. The presence and relative importance of each component will inevitably vary from person to person.

What is appropriate data on which to base a decision? As has been said before, there is no way that what you might consider suitable criteria can be given here – this is, simply, because all individuals must consider the issues, and decide what is appropriate for them. For example, some people may feel it is important to be aware of the effect of decisions they make on others:

> Jo was given the chance to work on a fascinating programming problem which aimed to revise an existing machine management programme, largely by automating processes under central control. Further information revealed that the effect of successful implementation would be to make over 50 people redundant. Despite the professional attractions, Jo felt unable to continue working on this project.

The issue is not whether Jo was right or wrong to take that decision, but that she was aware of the importance *to her* of the possible redundancies. Another person, holding different views, might well have reached a different decision. For personal reasons, it happened that Jo felt strongly about unemployment. The important point is that she was aware of this, and of other issues she considered relevant, and was able to apply them consciously in reaching a decision – in this case, whether or not to continue her involvement in the project.

Determining what is important to you in this way is clearly something only you can do, so it really is vital that you spend time working out your beliefs. Incidentally, the process is best not delayed – it is often easier to reach a decision on your views if you are able to do so *before* facing problems.

A final example:

> Martin works for a large business. Some time ago, he was asked to 'quietly' gather information which would, potentially, allow management to modify production software. The object was to allow continued production, even if various sections of their workforce were on strike. Martin was offered a bonus, and decided to go ahead. He doesn't know what use was made of the data.[3]

In Martin's case the eventual result was different from Jo's, but, despite their very different conclusions, the process of evaluation each carried out was similar.

How do we decide?

The following points are also referred to in the next chapter, which looks at ways of resolving ethical issues. Headings in this section should help in identifying areas which need more detailed consideration; what you consider to be most important will depend on you. A personal 'filter', discussed earlier, of course depends upon this information.

The first and most important indication that a decision may involve ethical issues is, unfortunately, the most difficult to describe. It deals with the particular effects that problems may have on individuals, and the ways in which a subconscious 'opinion' can make itself felt. How can this be done? It would be possible to write pages of definition, but in the final analysis it is best to trust your own perceptions. I would suggest, then, that if a decision or task does not *feel* right, it is almost certainly worth examining the issue more deeply.

This 'not feeling right' may have several visible effects. Often, it may result in your attempting to avoid the issue altogether. If it is considered, though, the feeling of concern may well result in your being reluctant to discuss the problem with others. This might encourage you to take a dogmatic stand, in order to head off any risk of being questioned or challenged. Alternatively, it could mean the opposite – you might spend considerable time in asking other people's opinions, hoping that they will provide you with the confidence to continue. Whatever symptoms you may personally display, behind them, probably recognized only by you, will be the uncomfortable feeling that something is wrong.

It is important not to ignore this feeling, but equally important to tackle it constructively. Once the need to examine an issue or problem further is identified, probably the best way to move forward is to perform some sort of structured analysis.

The following gives some idea of how a problem with ethical implications might be examined.

Effects of the issue

First, consider how the issue may affect others:

- How does the issue affect others *practically?*
- How does the issue affect others *emotionally?*
- How does the issue affect others *morally?*

These are three key aspects; looking at them should help you to decide whether this is an issue having wider effects. However, it is not only others who may be affected.

How does the issue affect you?

- How does the issue affect you *practically?*
- How does the issue affect you *emotionally?*
- How does the issue affect you *morally?*

The next aspect of a problem to consider is one of *size*. Given that we wish to be practical, it is reasonable to discover how much energy may be needed to solve the problem, or to resolve the issue.

Becoming involved in an issue may commit you to taking a stand, and this may in turn involve much else. For some people, it is important to always be prepared to take on big organizations and even governments. Our campaigning organizations are led and supported by such committed people. Others prefer to limit their involvement to actions where they feel there is a realistic chance of achieving their wishes, within a reasonable time-scale; you must decide where on the line you are (Figure 3.3). Of course, your exact position may, and almost certainly will, vary with each issue.

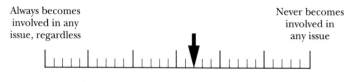

Figure 3.3 Where on the scale are you?

Richard was employed by a software company which had subcontracted nuclear power-related work. Richard felt very strongly that safety issues were being given too low a priority. Not content to tell his management and request a move to other work, Richard 'went public' and told the press.

If the problem is felt to be appropriate for analysis, and is of a size to be taken on, the next stage is one of *identification*. This may be expressed as, 'is this the issue, or is it just a symptom?', where a larger problem is seen only in terms of its effects; or, perhaps, 'is this the issue, or is it really something broader?', where the perceived problem is really one aspect of a much wider issue. It is important to make sure that you have correctly identified the whole of the problem, rather than assuming that a fin represents the whole shark...

Bill wanted a new colour monitor. He was particularly unhappy because a colleague in the next office had been given one, and he had not. However, when the position was looked at more closely, it was found that company policy – unchanged since colour monitors were *very* expensive – only allowed the purchase of one monitor a section in a financial year. Pure luck had brought his colleague's name to the top of the list. Once management was aware of changed circumstances, policy was changed. Bill (and the rest of his group) got new monitors.

Conclusions

This chapter has looked at what an 'ethical' problem in computing might be and how such problems may be identified. After looking briefly at the background to ethical discussions, this chapter examined some typical problems in the field of computing, and discussed how they might be defined and what they might involve. It suggested that computing was not a separate area, and stressed the importance of transferring accepted standards of behaviour to computing, as well as deciding on what made 'computer-specific' problems. The dynamic nature of computing technology was discussed, together with the importance of appreciating that the development of technology can easily outpace ethical development. Examination of what makes an ethical issue followed, with discussion on the way a cognitive 'filter' may be constructed to bring potential problems to the surface for discussion. Finally, the conclusion that 'not feeling right' about an issue was a good indicator of whether it merited examination was reached, and the chapter ended with a suggested list of headings to facilitate analysis.

Questions

1. Have you previously come across work-related ethical issues? Has the reading of this chapter given you any fresh views on them?
2. Suggest three criteria which might be used to define what you would consider to be an ethical problem. Which is the most important, and why?
3. Do you feel you already have an ethical code? If so, where do you think it has come from?
4. Can you think of any external events which have altered your beliefs?
5. Where on the campaigning scale do you feel you are? Why?

Notes

[1] Athough based on actual examples, to protect confidentiality, identifying details have of course been changed.
[2] For the purpose of this discussion I define an 'opinion' as a view which is lightly held, which is open to debate, and which may change. A 'belief' is deeply held, is seldom open to debate, and is unlikely to change.
[3] However, do you think he should have enquired? Why?

4

Reaching decisions

This chapter moves on from the task of identifying an ethical problem to examining ways of deciding what to do about it. It includes examples of 'ethical' problems and decisions, and looks at both the immediate relevance of resolution, and potential 'knock-on' effects. Practical discussion on how people reach decisions, including external and internal pressures to respond in a fixed manner, is also included.

The previous chapter suggested several ways in which issues might be identified as 'ethical'. The concept of ethical codes was defined as individual; so the approaches discussed looked at the specific relationship between an issue under analysis, and the personal standards of conduct of the concerned individual. It is of course this inter-relationship, between personal view and potential problem, which defines what an individual feels to be an 'ethical' issue.

Think it through

However, it is obviously not sufficient simply to identify an issue as appropriate for ethical consideration and then to do nothing further. The important task of identifying a problem is an essential stage, but merely a first step in the process of defining an appropriate response. Once a problem is identified, it is necessary to decide what to do about the issue, and, specifically, how the person concerned should actually proceed. Such a focused decision process, because it is, ultimately, closely centred on a person's basic convictions, will inevitably test both the individual and the individual's beliefs. For this reason, most people find that the next stage in the process is usually the most difficult one.

Faced with a problem defined and accepted as having an ethical component, what should be done next?

Avoidance is itself a decision

The first and most important point for a person in this position to establish is that a decision will be reached *whatever* you do. Walking away from a problem is, consequently, just as much 'making a decision' as is resolving to become involved. This point is often quite difficult to grasp, particularly as many of us might in the past have found it much easier to 'deal' with difficult issues by simply not thinking about them. However, ignoring the problem is emphatically not an appropriate answer. Sticking your head in the sand by deciding not to think about an issue is, effectively, just another, and much less honest, method of deliberately walking away from it.

Let me stress that, by making this point, I am not arguing that it is always essential to take action on ethical issues, or even that it is always necessary to become personally involved in them. With every issue you have identified as 'ethical' normally comes a whole range of possible options, and the only really essential action is to be sure that you have adequately considered all of them. It may well be, after careful consideration, that you do finally decide that it is appropriate to leave that issue alone. As a *conclusion* to your analysis, this would be perfectly acceptable; but it is a poor starting point.

The fundamental issue to understand is that whatever an appropriate action may turn out to be, the primary need is for analysis to take place *before* a conclusion is reached. Only if the result of this analysis gives endorsement to 'walking away' from the problem, does that action become appropriate. Until then, it is an unacceptable retreat.

A basic difference between these two routes to the same decision is, of course, that a conclusion which has been reached after 'thinking through' a situation is likely to be better founded than behaviour which was simply reactive, and which followed no clear plan.

It is also true that a decision which has been reached after careful consideration is more likely to be one with which you feel personally comfortable. Quite apart from other advantages, the knowledge that all possible courses of action have been considered and evaluated is, in itself, reassuring. Knowing that every option genuinely has been carefully evaluated must certainly leave less room for nagging doubts – doubts which sometimes follow even the most sensible decisions.

Whatever the eventual outcome may be, the process of 'thinking through' an issue is consequently the first step to take.

Arguing backwards

Another typical mistake made by those confronted with the need to resolve an ethical issue is 'arguing backwards'. I define 'arguing backwards' as a distorted reasoning process, which takes place only in order to justify a desired action. The process works by allowing you to convince yourself that appropriate analysis of an issue is taking place. However, what is actually happening is, instead, a deliberately confusing process, from which justifications emerge to support a decision which has already been reached.

Here is a typical example, based on a composite of several cases:

> A busy programmer is faced with an old, much-modified routine that possibly needed recoding. Examining the position in depth would probably provide unwelcome news and unwanted work, so their 'analysis' of the situation looked only for reasons that the code might be left as it was.

Such a distorted approach is to be avoided for several reasons. First, it is intellectually dishonest and calculated to deceive others, as well as – just as importantly – yourself. Secondly, decisions reached in this way are unlikely to be satisfactory. Finally, at best it merely postpones the need for a proper resolution of the issue.

It is also true that behaving in this way undermines and ultimately invalidates the whole analytic process. 'Analysis' then becomes a sham, giving spurious justification for actions which were already decided – or spurious justifications for inaction, of course. This point is an important one, as the process of analysis itself is a pivotal element in the successful resolution of ethical problems.

Again, this is not to suggest that the desired conclusion was necessarily inappropriate. On the contrary, it might well turn out to be perfectly suitable. However, whether the code actually needed rewriting or not is really irrelevant to the process of analysis. In order for a choice to be well founded, it is *essential* that any decision comes after, and not before, the analytical process.

Summary

Before moving on to consider ways of tackling a problem, let us summarize the main points from material in this section.

1. When faced with the need to tackle an 'ethical' issue, it is essential to begin by thinking through possible actions, and their likely results.
2. Refusing to consider the issue *is* taking action.
3. The *process of analysis* is central to the decision-making process. Whether or not the eventual outcome is identical to the originally anticipated outcome is irrelevant.

Tackling a problem

Once an individual has decided to think through an issue which potentially has ethical implications, there are various resources that may be available to helping resolve problems. As a first stage in examining these, it may help to begin by following an example which illustrates several of the related issues.

Let us assume we have been presented with a problem similar to that faced by Jill:

Jill worked for a small commercial software house specializing in financial systems. A software engineer since leaving university, two years earlier, she enjoyed her job and was good at it.

Although until then she had worked in one office, Jill had been asked by her boss, Ian, to agree to be briefly seconded to another company, apparently to help them finish an overdue project. She would continue to draw salary from her firm, who would in turn charge for her services.

Jill agreed, moved to the other company, and for two weeks worked there. Ian then unexpectedly asked for a 'frank' report on the new company, together with a complete dump of the software on which she was working. He told her she must 'keep very quiet' about it.

Jill felt she had been placed in an impossible situation. Her work for the new firm had gone well, and she had rapidly been accepted there as one of a team. On the other hand, she also felt loyalty to her own company, and to her boss, Ian. Nevertheless, she was very uncomfortable about his request. Quite apart from her conflicting professional feelings, she needed to feel able to 'live with herself', as she later described it. The software clearly did not belong to her boss, but it also felt wrong to pass on, to an outsider, information she had gained from new colleagues, who had welcomed her to their team ....

There are a number of issues involved here. First, there is the questionable legality of Ian's request for a tape of the software. Even though it was partly written by his employee, ownership must surely be with the company which developed it – after all, they paid the production costs. The request for a discrete report, though, is more difficult to deal with. Unless Ian had made it clear why it was wanted – and he had not – there are few obvious indicators to help Jill decide what to do.

Once the facts, including the legal position, are clear, it is for Jill to decide what is important to her, and consequently what actions could be supported. Only Jill is qualified to decide what factors are appropriate ones for her to consider, but some issues which might be relevant include:

- The trust given Jill by her new team
- Their possible reactions if they knew about her secret role
- What use might be made of information if she should decide to provide it
- What effects her response (whatever it may eventually be) might have
- Her relationship with her boss
- The consequences for her future career and, of course, Jill's own feelings about being used in this way.

What help is available?

First, of course, Jill needs to think through how the actions her boss suggested she take fit with her own ethical standards. As we have said, ethical standards are individual, and different people may therefore respond to the same circumstances in different ways. However, it is likely that a request to, in effect, steal a tape of newly developed software would immediately show up as a problem for most people. Other points might be more difficult to resolve without help, though.

Professional codes

Assuming her preliminary examination of the proposed actions showed a need for more information or help, Jill might then consider looking at her professional organization's Code of Conduct – such professional codes are discussed in detail in Chapter 7.

Reference to a formalized professional code can normally assist in three main ways:

1. Firstly, reference to a code may help to identify both current and future problem areas. This is particularly useful in identifying potential ethical issues, and so encouraging working to resolve them *before* they become actual problems.

2. Secondly, because a formal code has been developed and agreed by an entire profession, simply by its existence it extends justification and support to individuals faced with problems covered by the code – 'I realized then it wasn't just me being difficult', as one individual has described it.

   Jill may have been supported, for example, by the BCS (British Computer Society) Code, which says, 'Members shall have due regard to the legitimate rights of third parties'.

3. Thirdly, once an issue has been identified as breaching a professional code, it may allow both direct and indirect help in *resolving* the problem from the professional body itself.

As is discussed in Chapter 7, it makes sense for computing professionals who belong to organizations such as the BCS to familiarize themselves with their professional code, even before meeting a source of conflict. Knowledge of what the code says may permit general problems to be headed off, before they are experienced.

Other professional support

Although reference to a professional code is important, there are of course additional sources of support and advice. Talking through the situation with other people can be of considerable help, for example, both in deciding whether an issue is important enough to act upon, and deciding what action is appropriate.

It is important, though, that this sort of discussion is viewed by those taking part principally as an opportunity to help the person concerned consider the issues involved, and to support that person in exploring the implications of various courses of action. It is emphatically *not* an opportunity from a safe seat on the sidelines, to tell someone what they should do.

Jill may also be able to discuss matters with colleagues or fellow professionals. She might learn from them ways that situation could be handled, perhaps based on local experience. Often, what quite understandably appears to the person concerned to be a unique and worrying case is actually a replay of an earlier problem which had been satisfactorily resolved.

The important point is that the chance to talk freely about a problem, and your perceptions of it, to people who understood the technical background can be of considerable help. The circumstances of this particular example obviously made discussion with colleagues awkward, though.

Personal support

Professional information may come from codes of conduct, and informed discussion can take place with colleagues and fellow professionals, but it is vital to remember there is also a human dimension to most ethical issues – a personal, emotional one.

Until ethical problems are actually experienced, their emotional side may easily be overlooked. Particularly when considering ethical issues academically, it is rather too easy to look at examples as modern morality plays, unreal situations involving puppets rather than people. In reality, the need to face an ethical decision – however clear-cut it may be – is likely to be emotionally very draining.

It is important to bear in mind that there is always a natural compulsion to reduce or remove such emotional burdens. The pressure to do so, by avoiding any sort of confrontation, may be considerable.

Support from family and friends can play a major part here. Far from being a mistake to bring 'work' problems home, the knowledge that you are supported in your beliefs and decisions by your family can be a considerable source of strength. Talking things through, with someone who is known to be 'safe' or 'on your side', is secure, as well as supportive. A full understanding of the situation also helps a partner who is relied upon to provide emotional comfort.

Of course, families are not simply passive providers of encouragement; it is important not just to consider yourself, but those who may depend upon you. A person faced with an ethical problem therefore has an additional responsibility: to be sure that members of his or her immediate family are aware of what may be happening, and are allowed to contribute their views to help toward the eventual decision. The ethical reasons to do so are obvious: 'If a desire to avoid compromising my beliefs will result in my partner and children going hungry, have I the right to act without consulting them?'

Particularly if there are dependants, then, it is not sufficient for individuals to consider themselves in isolation. It is important that a family is always given the opportunity to be involved in discussion, even if they are likely to disagree. Concealing the position from a partner through fear of their reaction, although understandable, is not a long-term solution to any problem.

Resolution

In this case, Jill was able to draw on various sources of support, including her professional organization, to define what she felt was appropriate for her to do. She did not provide a copy of the software, but did produce a written report. Before doing so, though, she consulted her new colleagues, and made sure they knew what she was doing, and were aware in advance of the report's contents. Probably the most disturbing thing of all for Jill was the reaction of her boss, Ian. Faced by Jill with a detailed and supported response to his request, he claimed to have been 'only trying it on', and had no real need for the information. Jill has since changed her job.

In summary, then, there are a number of different ways in which 'the problem' may be resolved into 'what to do'. These must start and finish with the individual beliefs of the person concerned, but there are ways in which help and support can be provided.

Faced with an ethical problem:

- Consider your own ethical standards and beliefs. Does this show that the issue needs resolution?
- Consider appropriate professional standards, and, in particular, any relevant code of conduct. Does this show a case exists, as well as, perhaps, offer potential support from your professional organization?
- Consider talking things through with informed colleagues or other professionals. It may help put matters in perspective.

And finally

- Do not overlook emotional and practical support from family and friends.
- If your friends and family will be affected by your decision, make sure that they have an opportunity to be involved in the decision process.

What can discourage ethical behaviour?

Once the process of identifying an issue as having ethical implications is over, and a decision reached on what to do, there are still potential hurdles to be crossed. Although it would be very pleasant to say that ethical actions are always possible and are always rewarded, this is unfortunately not true. Particularly when working with others, a computer scientist may find that, far from being welcome, an ethical stance may uncomfortably remind their colleagues of what they would prefer to forget.

> Ganesh joined a research team working within a large company, and rapidly found that unrealistically long periods were allowed for software development. Ganesh, eager to make a good impression, worked late and hard, and turned in his first piece of work a week early. Far from being impressed, his team leader looked on Ganesh as a troublemaker, whose productivity was showing up the poor standards of other workers.

In this case, Ganesh was confused. He had been working in a way that he felt was appropriate, and had expected that his efforts to do well would be appreciated. To fit in with the conflicting – and lower – standards of his new team, he was faced with compromising what he felt right. His team leader may seem to us to be clearly in the wrong, but Ganesh's knowledge of that would not make her very much easier to work with.

Although not directly related to the use of computers, Sue's problem illustrates the difficulty of having to work within an unofficial 'office culture', a culture which may be personally unacceptable.

> Sue found the cosy arrangements in her office hard. Her colleagues (who needed to visit clients all over the UK fairly often) had a tradition of claiming an extra £5 on travel and hotel expenses. The money was put in a pot, and spent on things like office parties and theatre trips. Sue felt this was wrong, and refused to participate. Although clear about her own views, and sure she was right not to become involved, she was uncertain whether it would be appropriate to tell anyone in authority about the scheme.

Apart from difficulties with colleagues and managers, there are practical issues which can affect your decisions. In an ideal world, no one would be compelled to do what they felt wrong; but it is by no means uncommon for cases such as Mike's to occur:

> Mike had been unemployed for some time. A local business had recently been taken over, and the workforce – including computer staff – offered reduced salaries. An industrial dispute followed. The company advertised for new staff, and, after much thought, Mike applied for and got a job there. He had to cross picket lines every day, and 'felt terrible', but believed his family needed the money.

There can be no right and wrong answers to ethical problems like these. It is really only possible to make a correct decision if you are actually in the situation, and even then 'correct' can only reflect what you yourself feel is appropriate, rather than any kind of absolute answer.

The important thing for Mike, for example, was that he had thought through the situation *before* taking action. It would, of course, have been much easier just to think about the money he could earn, and not about the wider issues. Mike's decision was to apply for the job, but also to make a regular contribution to the strike fund. To us this may seem rather puzzling, but for Mike it was an appropriate answer, an answer which made him comfortable with his eventual decision.

Pressures

Pressures to act in a certain way may come from our friends, too; behaviour which is accepted by them as appropriate is often very difficult for us to reject. We feel that they will see us as appearing to be rejecting them, rather than their actions.

> Peter, who was unmarried, liked to go in to his office on Saturday afternoons to work quietly on a long-term project. He was sometimes visited there by friends. One asked to use the telephone, but this quickly escalated, and Peter found to his horror that international calls to America and beyond were being made. Peter did not feel it was right to allow this, and said so, but his friends found his refusal hard to appreciate. 'After all, it doesn't cost you anything.' Rather than argue, Peter gave up going to the office on Saturday.

It may be easy to condemn Peter for not being more open and for not telling his friends to leave the telephone alone. We would surely have been more outspoken. Nevertheless, the pressures on Peter were strong – it is surprisingly hard to challenge the views of our friends.

Finally, pressures on us from the attitudes and views of our family can affect our ability to act ethically and to take decisions which we may otherwise feel appropriate. It is important to try to distinguish between different sorts of family pressures, though. As a single teenager, there is an inherent need to demonstrate independence and maturity. Resisting the pressure of parents to act in a way which is acceptable to them is understandable, if sometimes unwise – learning by making mistakes is a part of becoming an adult. However, if, later in life, an action you propose could result in demotion, or losing a job, or even possible legal action, it is unreasonable to bring this upon a partner without very solid justification.

The process of ethical decision-making

It is now time to bring together the various points and issues which have been discussed so far, and to combine them into a practical method of reaching decisions on ethical problems.

Consider the flow chart, shown in Figure 4.1. This shows the steps which can be taken to identify an ethical problem, and brings together the points we have discussed, as well as identifying some additional stages which can help in focusing on the problem, and in reaching an appropriate solution.

Most of the points discussed have already been dealt with in this chapter, but one of the last stages, 'Scale', is new. This item is intended to identify what can be *realistically* tackled by an individual. It is sometimes surprisingly easy to slide gradually into a situation where taking an ethically appropriate stand may result in considerable individual problems, without there actually being very much hope of making any realistic changes to the circumstances. Clearly, the ethical state of a problem is not affected by the degree of difficulty involved in responding to it. Nevertheless, it may be important to keep a degree of realism in mind, too.

For example, as a hard-pressed but ethical computer scientist, you may find it unethical for the government to spend a percentage of your income tax on maintaining a Data Protection Registrar. In this view you may or may not be right. However, it is unlikely that, as an *individual*, you

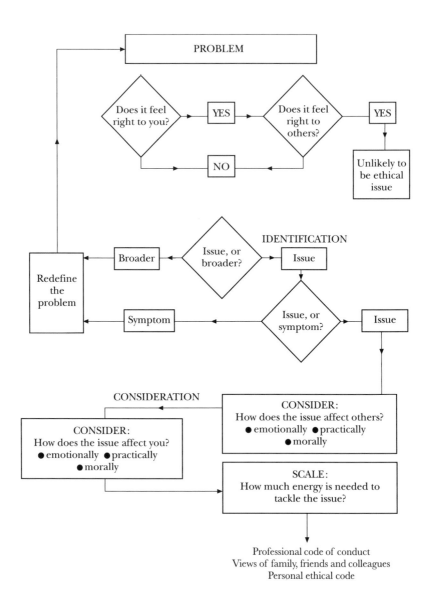

Figure 4.1   Process of ethical decision making

alone will be able to achieve a change. Your energies may therefore actually be better spent in pursuing a more achievable goal. Again, this view does not discount the possibility of your deciding, despite these difficulties, that it is appropriate to take on the government single-handed; but it does mean that, before doing so, you should have thought through the implications, including the demands it may make on you, and the limited likelihood of success.

Conclusions

Several general points were considered in this chapter. Avoidance of a potentially worrying situation is understandable, but walking away from a problem seldom resolves it. The need is for analysis to occur before a decision is taken – and, of course, although this may not be immediately obvious, avoidance is itself a decision.

False analysis was also discussed – the example given being 'arguing backwards', or seeking supposedly justified reasons for actions which have already been decided. This was doubly inconsistent, as not only would the eventual 'decision' then be likely to be flawed, but the practice of false analysis itself undermines the whole analytic process. This is potentially disastrous, as the process of analysis is central to the resolution of ethical problems.

Probably the most important issue was the constantly stressed need to thoroughly 'think through' the implications and background to an ethical issue, and to reach a final decision with which you are comfortable. It is emphatically *not* enough to discontinue the process immediately an issue has been identified. Realistically, until a decision has actually been made, nothing has been achieved.

The analytic process ideally draws not only upon the ethical standards of the concerned individual, but is assisted by both professional and personal support.

Some pressures which may work against ethical resolution were mentioned next – the need to be seen as reasonable by friends and colleagues, the influences of our family.

Finally, the chapter concluded with a flow chart illustrating a model of the ethical decision-making process.

Questions

1. Confronted with a problem which is clearly 'ethical', would you deal with it yourself, or discuss it with someone?
   Who? And why would you choose them?
2. What part do you think that a professional organization should play?
3. 'No problem is too big to run away from.' How justified do you feel this statement is in relation to ethical issues?
4. Is the answer to ethical problems usually pretty clear?
   How necessary do you think problem analysis really is?
5. If you were in the same situation as 'Jill', what do you think *you* would have done?

5

Specific problems

This chapter examines areas where working with computers can throw up obvious and not so obvious ethical problems, and looks in detail at some.

Even if, before looking at this book, you felt you knew nothing of the subject, by now you should be feeling reasonably able to spot an ethical problem. Although the details of the law and formal support systems are yet to come, how to attempt to identify an ethical issue and reach an appropriate solution should be becoming clearer.

This chapter, under a series of headings, looks at a variety of ethical problems which have affected different people working with computers. Naturally, the range of possible ethical issues within the field of computing is wide, so the intention here is to do no more than demonstrate some of the variety of potential problems. Illustrating the different ways in which individuals actually reacted has generally been avoided, as it is important to understand there are no definitive 'right' ways to respond.

A selection of 'typical' questions from within the computing field are examined in turn. Although these issues are certainly not intended as an exhaustive list, they do cover many likely problem areas.

What is an ethical problem?

As we have seen, an ethical problem expresses the conflict between the demands and pressures of a given situation and the values of a concerned individual. This conflict may show itself by making you feel uncomfortable, or perhaps uneasy. For the purposes of this chapter, a good working definition, as opposed to a technical definition, of an ethical problem is 'a problem which makes you feel uncomfortable, either in the proposed solution or in the particular circumstances surrounding the problem itself'.

Problems involving people

It is sometimes easy to forget that many computing problems are not related to actual software and hardware development; some difficulties come about at a much earlier stage. A good example lies in the interaction between a systems analyst and the commissioning client.

> Noreen had been asked to prepare an analysis of the needs of a transport company for an integrated freight database. Her job was made more difficult by the client's reluctance to allow sufficient time for an adequate initial investigation – Noreen felt that because this work was not very 'visible', it was not properly appreciated.

The responsibilities of systems analysts are well established and clear-cut – essentially, they must translate user needs into technical specifications. It is therefore understandable that a client may look to a systems analyst to advise appropriately on what the technical requirements may be and how these might best be met. However, very few clients are content to allow analysts a free hand. It is quite likely, for instance, that there is an uneasy fit between the budget a client is prepared to make available and the facilities requested by potential users of the system. In these circumstances a need to 'cut the cloth to fit the purse' may conflict with an analyst's professional knowledge of what an underfunded implementation might involve.

> Donald was the senior member of an external team preparing analysis of the data processing needs of a large corporation. The task was interesting and enjoyable, but it became obvious that there was a large gap between what the team felt would be necessary and what could realistically be funded. Donald was under considerable pressure from his company to gain a contract, but no system he could recommend or design was able to do the job adequately for a low enough price.

Donald is caught between two incompatible objectives. What should he decide? The client understandably anticipated that he would make an appropriate professional recommendation which could be implemented; his company expected him to do all that he could to land a substantial contract.

The 'contract landing' aspect of the problem was particularly important, because, if he did not succeed in obtaining contracts, the future for Donald and his firm would surely be bleak.

Although it is true that he owes a duty to his employer, Donald surely owes a stronger duty to a client who is trusting his professional judgement. There are practical, as well as ethical, reasons why this is important. If an implementation which proved defective or inadequate were recommended, for example, the consequences could well be serious. Most importantly, though, Donald owes a duty to himself. Specifically, he must keep in mind the concept of what, for him, is appropriate behaviour, and only depart from it after full consideration of the consequences.

It would be misleading to suggest that Donald's eventual decision would be either right or wrong. Like most other cases discussed in this chapter, there is no simple resolution to this problem. Different people in Donald's shoes might react differently. Faced with conflicting professional demands, what criteria should *you* use to help come to a decision? Certainly the views of employers, client, and yourself; but the decision on what other factors to include, together with the weight to be given to each, must always be an individual one.

Consider another typical case involving a systems analyst, where the ethical problem is less obvious.

> Gill was discussing needs with potential users of a new system. Although she wanted to take their views appropriately into account, there was no doubt that some of the user requests would involve much more work than others. The users knew little of technical realities; it would consequently be very easy to persuade them something was not technically possible, rather than admitting that it was merely difficult or expensive.

It is perhaps unusual for a such a situation to be formally examined in this way. Analysts, such as Gill, who are confronted with such requests normally decide what to do immediately, on an incident by incident basis. Officially, very few systems analysts would admit that they ever discourage users from requesting unwelcome features, yet the practice is certainly not unknown.

Of course, it is also easy to visualize Gill's problem in reverse. Sometimes there may be a tempting solution, technically very attractive, but which may not actually be in the best business interests of a client.

As always, when confronted with similar situations to these, it helps to have considered in advance likely questions, together with possible options and reactions. For example, one possible answer to Gill's difficulty would be to list all such 'difficult' requests for later vetting by more senior members of the client firm. Not only might they be technically more informed, but, if convinced the request is appropriate, they will be in a better position to justify increased expense. In normal circumstances it is best to be open about technical problems; blinding clients with science is not recommended.

Problems involving software

'Release the beta; that'll show up any bugs' – traditional.

Not all potential difficulties directly involve other people. The increasing power and widespread application of both computer systems and software mean that a decision taken by a software engineer may well have social implications, which understandably might not have been considered in a purely technical analysis. There is a continual need to keep an appropriate perspective on technical implementations without compromising the *effect* of its use by non-specialists.

As one database design professional put it:[1]

There is a struggle between efforts to provide straightforward access to networked services and databases, yet a need to keep sensitive data secure. The conundrum is that as the personnel needing such data are more valuable/educated (e.g. doctors), the more sensitive the data and the LESS likely the users are to want to fuss with yet another password/access limitation. I work in a teaching hospital, where no one wants to have to log out of their sessions connecting them to the clinical laboratory blood workups, on physically accessible terminals, much less remember a password.

While this seems like an interface or data security problem (and one that can be solved with hardware such as strip readers, software time-outs, etc.), and not a database problem, the fact is, it will often be up to the database designer what fields to cross-index on, what kind of information the application managers need to know, how much the application designers need to know, how much the end users are allowed to see, etc. Throw in the wild card of open systems, and the mix does become an ethical problem: I know what my team leader is telling me to provide, but I am also aware of issues of liability (legal OR moral) in providing what is requested of me.

However, it is not only those people who actually work with and use computer systems who need to be carefully considered when development is being planned. A frequently overlooked, but very much wider circle, consists of those individuals whose lives may be affected by the outcome of systems design and implementation. These people may not themselves have had even indirect contact with the designers at any stage of system development, even though they may personally be greatly affected by it.

Unanticipated technical problems

COMPUTERS PAID BILLS
AS WOMAN LAY DEAD FOR 3 YEARS[2]

An example of what can happen when technical issues are considered in isolation occurred in 1993, when a bizarre case from Sweden was reported in the international press. It appeared that an elderly woman had, apparently, died in 1990, but lay undiscovered in her apartment for more than three years. During this time, 'computers received her pension and automatically paid her bills'. It was only after the landlord had made repeated efforts to gain the occupant's permission to renovate it that police were called to break into the apartment, and discovered the body. Presumably, had the landlord not wished to renovate the home, the automated pension and bill payment might have continued indefinitely.

A further example of the potential for problems lies in the interface between marketing and software development. A software developer may well feel that more time is needed to produce dependable software, while the commercial pressures on a marketing department are likely to push for an early release date. What does this mean for ethical software engineers, concerned that their software is predictable and reliable?

Doug was working on the development of an advanced software control package for industrial equipment. He was anticipating a further few months of development time, to provide him with an opportunity to 'shake the bugs out' of the system; but his company insisted on an early release. Signing off the development would, for Doug, imply he was happy with the state of the software; but he wasn't. His managers felt he was being unreasonable – after all, everything worked – and understandably wanted to realize some of the considerable sums invested in the project.

Who was really qualified to judge if the software was good enough to release – and what would happen if it was not? Doug surely had a point. On the other hand, the tendency of programmers to support 'creeping featuritis'[3] and reluctance to give up work on 'their' software, is proverbial. It is also true that Doug's company had to market software continually to survive. If no bugs were discovered – and none were obvious – three months would be wasted, and considerable profit lost.

The important issue here is not Doug's understandable (but perhaps unrealistic) wish to supply perfect software. In the 'real world' marketplace this is very seldom possible.

However, although equally understandable, neither should the commercial needs of a development company permit release of software before it is ready. Although financial pressures are often the most visible, the fundamental problem is conflict between the needs of those responsible for development of a program and the needs of those responsible for its marketing. For obvious reasons, tensions in this area are very common.

The issue in most such cases normally lies in deciding exactly where to draw the line, and how best to balance the conflicting needs of both standpoints. It is clearly important here for both sides to make positive efforts to appreciate and understand the other's case. In this instance, after discussion, a compromise was reached – Doug's ethical qualms meant he was allowed more time, although not nearly as much time as he had wanted.

The development of specialist software itself can also raise ethical problems. Consider the experiences of another database specialist, this time working in a setting with a clearly defined brief in ethical design:

> I was working on a database application that was to maintain circulation records for a library: which books are on loan, to whom, when they're due, whether there is a fine. The librarians were appropriately concerned that all information be secured against casual reading [by outsiders]. But they also taught me that transactional information, like books on loan, can and should be permanently discarded as soon as the transaction is dissolved (the book is returned). They argued that it is acceptable to increment descriptive counters for each transaction, and that it is justifiable to maintain some information that explains the source of any fines. But they were very concerned that information about an individual's reading habits should not be stored anywhere in the system, no matter what the security precautions.

It may well be useful to study the attitudes of other professions concerned with handling information. Librarians have a much more extensive experience than computer scientists in this area.

The growth of artificial intelligence systems offers another example of potential ethical problems. An 'intelligent' computer, or, more probably, a domestic or entertainment appliance driven by one, is likely to be available to a mass market soon. What decisions about its functions will have been made? Who will have been involved in advancing these criteria? The wider responsibilities of a development team are very real, even though a focus on features and other technical details may mean that other, less specific, issues have not have been considered in such depth.

Epstein's study package, 'The Case of the Killer Robot'[5] is an interesting application which illustrates the perils of too narrow a view. A detailed teaching scenario intended for class discussion, it combines elements of software engineering and computer ethics. The package consists of articles which discuss specific issues in both software engineering and computer ethics, such as programmer psychology, team dynamics, user interfaces, software process models, software testing, the nature of requirements, software theft, privacy and so forth. Interestingly, in view of earlier comments in this section, a major consideration of the package addresses the issue 'when is software good enough?'

> The articles in the scenario begin with the indictment of a programmer for manslaughter. This programmer wrote faulty code that caused the death of a robot operator. Slowly, over the course of many articles, the students are introduced to factors within the corporation which also contributed to the accident. Students (hopefully) begin to realize the complexity of the task of building real-world software and they begin to see some of the ethical issues intertwined in all of that complexity. They are shown software development as a social process.[6]

'The Case of the Killer Robot' certainly uses a fairly extreme example, but the lesson it gives, of the need to look beyond immediate issues to their possible effects, is certainly widely relevant. Growing links between commercial information systems; the spread of 'active badges' and associated computer tracking software; introduction of 'smart cards', as well as many other, less visible, technical developments, demonstrate clearly that the ethical computer scientist must be constantly aware of the social context surrounding technical issues.

Although the person concerned probably did not find it amusing, consider the classic case of a programmer who clearly did not bear in mind wider issues:

> The National Westminster Bank admitted last month that it keeps personal information about its customers – such as their political affiliation – on computer. But now

Computer Weekly reveals that a financial institution, sadly unnamed, has gone one better and moved into the realm of personal abuse. The institution decided to mailshot 2000 of its richest customers, inviting them to buy extra services. One of its computer programmers wrote a program to search through its databases and select its customers automatically. He tested the program with an imaginary customer called Rich Bastard.

Unfortunately, an error resulted in all 2000 letters being addressed "Dear Rich Bastard".

The luckless programmer was subsequently sacked.[7]

As a final example of the importance of the consideration of the broader effects computer software might have, consider the current development of virtual reality technology. Existing 'shoot 'em up' computer games software is widespread, but the psychological effects, both of repetitive playing and of counterfeiting such bloodthirsty activities, are not yet fully understood or explored. How much more important would be the submersion of an individual into a virtual reality simulation? What psychological effects might such an experience have, on the individual who undergoes it? Additionally, how might possible technical developments – laser images focused directly onto the eye, for example – affect an individual's physiology? Developers of virtual reality simulation must certainly be extremely skilled computer scientists – but there is perhaps a place on their team for someone concerned with the ethical implications of such development.

Although it may be impractical for every major new software and hardware development to undergo an 'ethics committee' vetting, in a similar way to the vetting that occurs in medical developments, there is surely a case to be made for fuller consideration of this issue.

Complex software

Let us now consider the question of highly complex software. The days are long gone when successful software was the product of a single, pizza-eating, coffee drinking programmer. Teams of software engineers now work to develop and maintain systems, and the resultant size and complexity of software is increasingly intimidating. Parts of existing software may be rewritten many times, and, in the words of the old saying, 'everybody's responsibility is no one's responsibility'. So: who is actually responsible if, when used in circumstances never foreseen by its original authors, a much-patched application develops problems? Who is ethically responsible if a newly developed complex piece of software fails?

Of course, it depends on the circumstances. Precise definition and delineation of responsibility in advance of problems is, however, indispensable. In particular, the way in which a programming team is structured is crucial. All members, including the team leader, need to have a clear perspective on the precise area of their responsibilities, and must be prepared to accept accountability for it. In order to do this, they need to be aware of the ways in which 'their' aspect of the project relates to other sectors, as well as to the overall project itself. Project managers, in addition to their normal activities, need to encourage and coordinate this delineation of responsibilities.

It is important to distinguish clearly here between legal and ethical responsibility; they may often go together, but this should never be assumed. A good distinction to keep in mind is that legal responsibility may be corporate, but ethical responsibility is always personal.

It is sometimes hard for those directly concerned to look beyond their immediate programming problem and to consider wider issues such as these. A programmer, explaining why she had not responded to a request for comments on security issues, may be expressing a common view:

> The topic sounds extremely interesting. I did not reply or post a response to the original question because I feel ignorant and did not have anything to say at the time. Maybe other interested folks are in the same position. It may be that most site programmers are not so interested in security issues because we want to keep our noses way down deep in the code and not deal with the unreal world. We are such an 'insecure' bunch…;-)

How then should work on a large program be handled? The responsibility of a programmer who is asked to work on revising a large program may be particularly tricky, for example. It is always more difficult to revise existing code rather than generating new. It may well be, too, that documentation and internal commenting of the existing code is inadequate. If this is so, it is then often impossible, without disassembling vast amounts of code, to know what all the parts of a program do. A further complication is that addition of new routines may or may not affect existing code, so, although all may appear well when working under test conditions, there may be no guarantee of freedom from later problems.

In these circumstances it would clearly be unreasonable to expect new programmers to assume ethical responsibility for the whole edifice. However, if they are not responsible, who is?

It is impossible to generalize; particular circumstances must affect cases in different ways. However, there are some basic assumptions which can be made. The most important of these is that every individual who contributes to software development must share overall ethical responsibility for the eventual product. It is not sufficient for anyone to concentrate on the task in hand and delegate *ethical* responsibility up the line. In this case, then, the ethical task of concerned programmers is not completed by just working to the best of their ability on their restricted areas of code. It is also necessary to relate individual work to the overall application, and to attempt to understand any relationship with larger issues.

A contrived example: a programmer is asked to modify a large database containing names and addresses. The client's intention is to allow automated generation of fake money-seeking charity letters. The letters will only be generated once the programmer has completed the task and left. Is it sufficient to produce a well-written database modification, or should the use to which it will be put be considered? Would the ethical issue be changed in any way if the programmer took a smaller role in the modification?

This is not, of course, to imply that large projects are inherently unethical, or even that they need special consideration. Such suggestions are clearly absurd. However, if the wider ethical consequences of a project do not seem personally relevant, and, especially, if a person's individual contributions to a project do not appear to have any immediate *effect*, there is a danger that inherent ethical problems will be obscured. Ethical distancing is clearly more likely when the sheer size of a project reduces the ability of individuals to feel they have made a meaningful contribution to the whole.

The more distant individual contributions become from the final product, the harder it becomes to identify a personal contribution as having any bearing on the whole. Essentially, the more extended and distant any effects of actions may be, the harder it becomes to recognize and acknowledge responsibility for them. One possible consequence of this distancing process may be that an individual becomes ethically detached. Their work on the project then seems to take place in an ethical limbo, where familiar rules do not apply.

In summary, here are some points which those who are concerned with the ethical issues involved in working on large projects should consider:

● The smaller a personal contribution is in relation to a final product, the more difficult it becomes to identify any ethical responsibility for it.

- Ethical responsibility is hard to define, and is therefore frequently ill-defined.
- Personal responsibility for 'your' part of the work may obscure the need for a share in responsibility for the project as a whole.

and, most importantly:

- Legal responsibility can be passed on. Ethical responsibility cannot.

Education may be the answer: general awareness of difficulties involved in the ethical management of large projects can go a long way to avoiding them.

Property rights

Strictly speaking, the question of intellectual property rights is a legal one, but there may sometimes be an ethical component, too. For example, consider the problems faced by Jay, a programmer with a large software developer.

Jay had an idea for the development of a business software package, and suggested it to his line manager. The idea was rejected, but Jay nevertheless worked on it after office hours and, sometimes, during lunch breaks. He was careful not to use 'company time'. However, when he finally showed a prototype, he was amazed that, although the idea was adopted, his work was taken over without compensation.

Jay felt his company had acted unethically – after all, he had not been paid for the development work, which of course had taken place in his own time. However, he had admittedly used his company's equipment. The issue was only finally settled when Jay re-read his contract. He discovered the contract made it quite clear: any software developed during the course of his employment automatically belonged to his employer. Such clauses are not at all unusual in company employment contracts.

Jay's experience emphasizes the importance of understanding the ground rules before claiming unethical conduct. If you have previously accepted a certain course of conduct as appropriate, it is unrealistic to claim later that it is unethical. Of course, it may be; but the time to identify it as unacceptable is when it is first presented – in Jay's case, when he initially saw a copy of the contract – rather than later, when the restriction actually becomes inconvenient.

Conclusions

This chapter has addressed a wide range of different problems, and has covered a variety of issues which have been perceived as 'ethical problems'. Although the cases were very different, several broader points emerged.

The first was the importance of clarifying the situation. What is involved, and what is your anticipated part in the issue? Without this information, it is impossible to develop an appropriate ethical response. The second point, which came from the section dealing with systems analysis, emphasized the need always to be aware of your responsibilities to both employer and client, but without losing sight of the importance of making an individual decision which reflects your ethical beliefs.

It is also important to respect the views of those who are less technically informed, and, in particular, to avoid 'blinding them with science'.

The fourth point was more general – it is essential to be prepared to consider the other person's point of view. Unless an issue is very important to you, always be prepared to compromise.

Fifthly, look out for wider, non-technical issues, and be aware of their importance. This consideration is particularly necessary when your contribution may only form part of a much larger whole.

Finally – you may be successful in transferring legal responsibility, but you cannot delegate or transfer your ethical responsibilities.

Questions

1. Should a client be entitled to expect systems analysts to put their personal views aside in the best interests of the *client* company?
2. Should an employer be entitled to expect systems analysts to put their personal views aside in the best interests of their *employing* company?

3. What weight do you think should be given to personal views in a business setting? Why?
4. If a client does not understand technical terms, is it their fault or yours? Does it actually matter?
5. Your boss says, 'Don't worry about the ethics – that's my job'. Are you relieved, or worried? Why?
6. How important to you is the way in which the outcome of your work may be used?

Notes

[1] A response to the request for professional database experiences, described in Chapter 10.
[2] From the *Los Angeles Times*, Sunday, 19 September, 1993.
[3] 'Creeping featuritis' is a condition of software development where, rather than sign off a project as completed, a programmer will continue to polish code indefinitely, often adding new and frequently unnecessary features.
[4] See the librarian's comments in Appendix C, for example.
[5] Available from `http://ricis.cl.uh.edu/FASE/Killer-Robot.html`
[6] Extract from introductory material, 'The Case of the Killer Robot'.
[7] *New Scientist*, 28 August 1993; Feedback column.

6

Legal constraints

All computing use is of course regulated by statute. This chapter looks at regulatory law within the UK, giving particular attention to the 1984 Data Protection Act and the 1990 Misuse of Computers Act.

Legislation

It is essential that those working within the computing field have a good knowledge of relevant legislation, although to some practitioners it may seem unnecessary or even irrelevant. The reason is simple – breaking laws can, and almost certainly will, cause difficulties; and ignorance of the law is no defence. In the event of problems, it has never been sufficient to claim unfamiliarity with the law. Knowledge of relevant legislation is particularly important if your personal code of ethics is in conflict with others. You certainly then need to understand exactly what is illegal, in order to decide if unlawful action may be appropriate, and, of course, to appreciate the possible consequences.

Although computing in the United Kingdom (UK) is in practice covered by a range of general legislation, there is also specialized law specifically relating to computer use. For all computer professionals working within the UK, some knowledge of the 1984 Data Protection Act and the 1990 Misuse of Computers Act is essential.

Even before the advent of specific computer-focused legislation, the use of computers was restricted by limitations enshrined in both international convention and UK law. For example, interchange of information is basic to the efficient use of computers. The European Convention of Human Rights, signed by the UK, explicitly states:[1]

1. Everyone has the right to respect for his private and family life, his home and his correspondence.

2. There shall be no interference by a public authority with the exercise of this right except such as is in accordance with the law and is necessary in a democratic society in the interests of national security, public safety or the economic well-being of the country, for the prevention of disorder or crime, for the protection of health or morals, or for the protection of the rights and freedoms of others.

However, legal boundaries are, naturally, more closely defined by legislative decisions, and these must inevitably reflect the views (and technology) of the period when the laws were passed. In other words, until the advent of specific computer-directed laws, existing legislation may have reflected an era of paper and typewriters, rather than electrons and terminals.

History

The introduction of all new technology can generally be argued to first imitate existing tasks, and only moving into new areas after these are met. For example, early printing technology first copied handwritten documents; the first cars closely resembled horse drawn carriages, and so on. It is understandable, then, that the first commercial computers were purchased and used to mechanize existing manual processes. (The unique, specialized applications – such as those which would have been impossible to implement manually – developed later.)

The differences between the original manual systems and the computer-based systems which replaced them were most visible in time-consuming labour-intensive activities. (Examples of the first manual systems to be 'computerized' were, of course, stock control and financial records.) The introduction of computers certainly greatly facilitated 'number crunching'. Their availability also drew attention to actions which, although feasible, had until now been both difficult and prohibitively expensive.

Any activity is legal unless specifically prohibited – the maxim, known to law students, is 'anything not forbidden is permitted'. Certainly, there had previously existed little purpose in legislating against activities which were only theoretically possible. New activities, which had not previously been considered by legislators, are consequently technically legal, even if they may be unethical. The spread of motor vehicles, far faster than horses, meant the eventual introduction of new laws restricting the speed of traffic. The plethora of computers allows the introduction of activities even less desirable than speeding.

Development of new legislation

When the use of computers was restricted to replacement of existing manual systems (and therefore to areas where the employment of manual systems had for many years been clearly understood) there were few problems. However, potential difficulties emerged when the second stage of development was reached in the 1960s, and computers began to undertake and accomplish tasks which had not previously been practical.

Consider, for example, the provision of credit references. It has of course always been possible to physically collect and store information about the credit-worthiness of an individual or company. Manual storage and subsequent analysis by hand of potentially huge volumes of relevant data is, however, difficult. Originally, although the results were of potential benefit to business, a credit-worthiness investigation was expensive, and therefore tended to be limited in scale. Indeed, formal credit references were largely confined to large businesses; for others, 'bank references' were commonplace. An individual's credit-worthiness was a simple function of the view the bank took of the person. Should an individual have no bank account, it was unfortunate.

The introduction of computer systems, and the subsequent development of commercial databases, dramatically changed this situation. Computers allowed private companies to build and, more importantly, search, hundreds of thousands of individual records. Information from many different sources could be collected, stored and collated – some data was understandably incomplete, some perhaps illegally obtained, and some just plain wrong. While similar data collection, using paper, had undoubtedly taken place in the past, the scale of manual systems was inevitably much smaller. For this reason, credit rating by manual systems had not generally been perceived as a problem.

In contrast, the use of computers meant it became simple to store and retrieve information. Personal references and material could readily be collated, extracted and sold, and credit agencies were soon formed expressly to supply such data.

As a simple illustration, assume we wish to find the exact address and personal details of Mr John Brown. We know he lives in a specific London borough, but no more. Since the 19th century, it has been possible to obtain a copy of an electoral register, and to examine it line by line, in this case looking for a match with Mr Brown. Even a small London borough may have some tens of thousands of electors; such examination would therefore take an impractically long time. In contrast, if the electoral register is available on-line, searching for a specific voter takes only seconds. It is so easy that searches might be made for trivial reasons. Lists of customers, creditors, bad credit risks and other such material may also be searched in a similar way.

The results of one search may be combined with other information: perhaps credit history as a customer of various companies, County Court judgements, responses to mailshots and so on. Building up detailed electronic pictures of individuals together with their personal circumstances – without them knowing anything about it – is quite practicable.

Incidentally, from an ethical viewpoint the use of improperly obtained data – for instance, data which had been provided specifically for one purpose, but used for another without the knowledge or consent of the person concerned – would normally be inappropriate, whether or not its use was illegal.

The case of John Brown is purely an example. Happily, few local authorities allow electronic sale of electoral register information, and, as is discussed later in this chapter, there are now legal restrictions on the collection, storage and access to personal data.

However, before legal restrictions, some computing practitioners did not appear to feel constrained by personal ethics. By the late 1970s and early 1980s there was increasing public disquiet about the uses being made of such personal data, both by computerized credit reference agencies and by others. This disquiet, together with European political pressure,[2] was the immediate precursor of the 1984 Data Protection Act.

This Act reflected the UK's desire both to counter the risk to individual privacy and to support the free international flow of information within Europe. Indeed, in the parliamentary debate on the Act (then a Bill), Lord Eton (Under-Secretary of State) said:

> The first [purpose] is to protect private individuals from the threat of the use of erroneous information about them, held on computers. The second is to provide that protection in a form that will enable us to satisfy the Council of Europe Convention on Data Processing so as to enable our own data processing industry to participate freely in the European market.

Although most attention has been given to its data protection components, this two-pronged approach – to encourage the use of international standards, and to protect the individual from incorrect entries on personal data – underlies the 1984 Act.

It is debatable whether the UK Government would actually have introduced legislation without a European lead; the 'freedom of information' aspect, for example, while popular in Europe, was certainly not given a high priority here.

Data Protection Act, 1984

The Data Protection Act was intended to stop misuse of computer files containing *personal data*. The concept of personal data is central to both the wording and operation of the Act, which, in Section 1, defines 'personal data' as:

> ... information which relates to a living individual who can be identified from that information (or from that and other information in the possession of the data user), including any expression of opinion about the individual but not any indication of the intentions of the data user in respect of that individual... which is recorded in a form in which it can be processed by equipment operating automatically in response to instructions issued for that purpose.

The Act says that, with certain exceptions, everyone holding personal information on a computer (significantly, manual systems were not included) must both operate within defined guidelines and additionally register their system and its data use with the Data Protection Registrar. It is the responsibility of the Registrar to ensure compliance with the Act.

Personal data is protected by the Act against three potential dangers:

- Against being incorrect, or incomplete, or irrelevant
- Against being distributed to unauthorized users
- Against being used for a purpose other than that for which it was collected

The Act's main sections attempt to provide this protection by stipulating that the storing and processing of personal data should be in accordance with the following eight principles:

1. The information to be contained in personal data shall be obtained, and personal data shall be processed, fairly and lawfully.

2. Personal data shall be held only for one or more specified and lawful purposes.
3. Personal data held for any purpose or purposes shall not be used or disclosed in any manner incompatible with that purpose or those purposes.
4. Personal data held for any purpose or purposes shall be adequate, relevant and not excessive in relation to that purpose or those purposes.
5. Personal data shall be accurate and, where necessary, kept up to date.
6. Personal data held for any purpose or purposes shall not be kept longer than is necessary for that purpose or those purposes.
7. An individual shall be entitled:
    (a) at reasonable intervals and without undue delay or expense:
        (i) to be informed by any data user whether he holds personal data of which that individual is the subject
        (ii) to access to any such data held by a data user;
    (b) where appropriate, to have such data corrected or erased.
8. Appropriate security measures shall be taken against unauthorised access to, or alteration, disclosure or destruction of, personal data and against accidental loss or destruction of personal data.

Although the comprehensive right of a subject to view, and, if necessary, correct, data which refers to him or her is defined, the Act does nevertheless have limits in its application. Sections 27 to 34 detail data which may be legally excluded from its provisions. Broadly, these begin by excluding anything viewed by any Minister as pertaining to 'national security' (S.27) and move on to exclude personal data:

- Held for 'Prevention or detection of crime', 'apprehension of offenders' and 'assessment of tax' (s.28,i)
- Held for 'Discharging statutory functions' (s.28,ii)
- 'Held by government departments or local authorities' for social work purposes (s.29)
- Held for the regulation of financial services (s.30)
- Held for the purposes of judicial appointments (s.31)
- Held for payroll and account data (with some restrictions) (s.32)
- Held for domestically held data (with some restrictions) (s.33)

Table 6.1   Example of personal data details

1984 Act Information – typical details

Purpose for collecting the data:
Personnel/Employee Administration

Types of individual about whom data is being held:

Current/past/potential   Current/past/potential retired persons
    employees
Trainees, voluntary workers

Classes of personal data held:

Academic record	Allowances, benefits, grants
Career history	Current employment
Current marriage or partnership	Details of other family/household members
Disabilities, infirmities	Financial identifiers
Health and safety record	Identifiers issued by public bodies
Immigration status	Insurance details
Licences, permits held	Marital history
Membership of committees	Membership of professional bodies
Payments, deductions	Pension details
Personal details	Personal identifiers
Physical health record	Professional expertise
Publications	Qualifications and skills
Racial, ethnic origin	Recruitment details
Termination details	Trade union, staff association record
Training record	Travel, movement details
Work record	

Other, specialized, exemptions are listed in s.34.

There are reservations about the contents of the Act – the omission of controls on paper documentation and the wide omissions relating to police- and government-held data are probably the most significant. However, the Act was undoubtedly a milestone.

It is important that subjects with personal information held on computer systems appreciate what information is held about them and for what purposes it is stored. There is both a legal and ethical responsibility for a data holder to make concerned people aware of these issues.

An organization must therefore collect information to comply with the legal requirements of the Data Protection Registrar, while at the same

Table 6.1 continued

Sources of data:

Data subjects themselves	Department of Education and Science
Department of Employment	Department of Health and Social Security employees, agents
Employers – past, current and prospective	Home Office
Inland Revenue	Trade unions, staff associations

To whom the data may be disclosed:

Banks	Building Societies
Data subjects themselves	Department of Education and Science
Department of Employment	Department of Health and Social Services
Education or training establishments, examining bodies	employees, agents
Employers – past, current and prospective	Home Office
Inland Revenue	Insurance companies
Local authority housing department	Local authority social services department
Survey or research organizations, workers	Trade unions, staff associations

time making the data subjects appropriately aware both that data collection takes place and of the uses to which information may be put.

The Open University provides an excellent example of good practice here. Appendix A contains a copy of the informative text given to all new Open University students, telling them about the storage of information concerning them and explaining the purposes for which it may be used.

A further check is made via the Data Protection Registrar; the questions posed by the Registrar to data holders are comprehensive and detailed. Some idea of this may be gained from Table 6.1, which shows typical question headings, together with the huge range of possible answers, which are required by the Data Protection Registrar under the 1984 DTP Act.

In sum: the 1984 Act lays a duty on most holders of electronic information which contains 'personal' data, information which concerns *people*. Such data must not only be held for a specific, legal purpose, but must be current and accurate. It may be checked and corrected by the person concerned, and the holder must register with the Data Protection Registrar, who polices compliance with the Act.

'Hacking'

However, computers are not just passive repositories of information. Particularly when connected to each other through a network, they are potential targets for attack, from a class of computer users known as 'hackers'. A hacker is someone who accesses a computer system without the express or implied permission of the owner. They may make such a connection remotely, by using a computer at home or office connected to a communications network, or directly, by accessing a computer through one of its terminals. (The ethics of hacking are discussed in Chapter 8.)

Hackers are not inevitably and automatically 'bad', and, although generally frowned upon by officialdom, hacking is not *necessarily* unethical. The vast majority of those considered to be hackers are probably enthusiasts, anxious to demonstrate their abilities, rather than malevolent anarchists determined to overthrow governments. However, it must be kept in mind that even the most innocent *unauthorized* access to a safety-critical computer system (such as flight control systems or hospital medical monitoring) may inadvertently create damage and risk to life, while at best, a path may be cleared for other, less innocent persons.

It had long been assumed in the UK that hacking (defined as the accessing of computer information without permission) was illegal; but in 1988 the House of Lords[4] eventually decided to the contrary. Concern following this decision led to the Law Commission Working Paper on Computer Misuse (HMSO, 1988). This paper, after a general examination of the problems, made several specific recommendations for changes in the law. In 1989 the Tory MP Emma Nicholson promoted a Private Member's Bill to combat hacking, but later withdrew it, following Government promises to legislate. However, despite these promises, no official Government measures were taken. In 1990 another private member, Michael Colvin, introduced a second private Bill on computer misuse. Although this Bill incorporated recommendations from the Law Commission paper, the penalties recommended by the Commission were greatly increased. The Bill eventually became the Computer Misuse Act in August 1990. As well as directly tackling the 'hacking' issue, Colvin's Bill took the opportunity to address other, wider problems concerning the use of computers.

Computer Misuse Act, 1990

The Act introduced three new criminal offences:

1. *Unauthorized access to computer material*
   Described by the Act's sponsor as 'simple hacking' – that is, using a computer without permission. This now carries a penalty of up to six months in prison or a £2000 fine, and is tried in a Magistrate's Court.
2. *Unauthorized access to computer material with intent to commit or facilitate commission of further offences*
   This section covers actions such as attempting to use the contents of an email (electronic mail) message for blackmail. This is viewed as a more serious offence; the penalty is up to five years' imprisonment and an unlimited fine.
3. *Unauthorized modification of computer material*
   This section covers distributing a computer virus, or malicious deletion of files, as well as direct actions such as altering an account to obtain fraudulent credit (or, perhaps, an increased examination grade).

Both items 2 and 3 are tried before a jury.

The Act also includes the offences of *conspiracy to commit* and *incitement to commit* the three main offences. This aspect of the Act makes even discussion of specific actions which are in breach of the main sections questionable practice. It is sufficient to be associated with an offender in planning the action, or to suggest carrying out an action which is illegal under the Act, to be in a position to be charged.

Finally, the Act attempts to cover international computer crime. An individual can be prosecuted in the UK under the 1990 Misuse Act as long as there is at least one 'significant link' with this country. For example, hacking into a computer in Milan from a terminal in London is illegal, as is hacking into London from Milan. Interestingly, using the UK as a staging post is also illegal under the Act – breaking into the Pentagon from Milan via a UK university is illegal, and could result in UK prosecution, even if the hacker had never been in England.

Interestingly, if a hacker (or anyone else) gains access to a system containing personal data, and then copies all or some of that data to their own system, they are likely to be guilty of breaking not just the 1990

Misuse Act, but also the 1984 Data Protection Act, as they will then be holding unregistered data. Even if they are registered, obtaining data 'knowingly or recklessly' is an offence.

Other legislation

There is a great deal of other legislation relevant to computer users in the UK. This includes:

- *For copyright issues:*
  The Copyright, Designs and Patents Act, 1988
- *For improper electronic claims – including for example the transfer of electronic funds:*
  The Forgery and Counterfeiting Act, 1981
  The Theft Act, 1968 (s.25)
- Trade Descriptions Act, 1968

For further information concerning these Acts and other legal aspects of computing (such as pornography issues, discussed in Chapter 8) reference to specialist books listed in the Bibliography on page 141 – for instance Bainbridge's *Introduction to Computer Law* – is strongly recommended.

Conclusions

Under UK law, it is illegal for most individuals and companies to hold personal data without safeguards. Those holding such data must be registered (with the Data Protection Registrar) and must ensure that the information they hold is correct. The data subjects may obtain copies of the data concerning them, and may correct it.

Data stored on a computer system is additionally protected from unauthorized access and alteration by the 1990 Computer Misuse Act.

Questions

1. Why should a computer scientist be concerned with computer law?
2. 'Existing laws are surely sufficient to cover computer use, too'. Why might this not be so?

3. What actions might a computer user take which (in your view) *ought* to be illegal? Why? Are any of these actions covered by existing legislation?
4. How is the storage of information on a computer system legally protected from unauthorized access?
5. Give some examples of unauthorized access to a computer system. What effects might such access have?

Notes

[1] European Convention of Human Rights, Article 8.
[2] European pressure culminated in the 1981 Council of Europe Convention on Data Protection.
[3] *Hansard*, Lords, 5th ser, v.443, col.509
[4] The House of Lords judgement concerned *R . v. Gold*, a famous case which arose from hacking the Duke of Edinburgh's Prestel mailbox.

7

Professional organizations and codes of conduct

The behaviour of those working with computers is, as described in Chapter 6, bound by statute. General computing practice is additionally enhanced by the codes of conduct issued by concerned professional organizations.

This chapter looks at formal professional codes of conduct, using the BCS (British Computer Society) and ACM (Association for Computing Machinery) codes as examples.[1] It also looks briefly at employers' common expectations concerning professional standards, and concludes with a detailed look at the BCS Code.

Professional codes

One of the definitions of a 'profession' is that it provides regulation of its members, and, in order to do so, defines appropriate standards of behaviour. Professional codes of conduct are the formal expression of these expectations and requirements, and all professional organizations normally make adherence to them a condition of membership.

It is, however, important to immediately stress that, because a code was drawn up by a particular body, it does *not* mean the contents of the code are of relevance only to members of that organization. Whether they are members of several organizations, or one, or none, everyone who works in the relevant field needs to be aware of what is considered appropriate behaviour. They also have a legitimate interest in knowing about attempts to codify it.

Of course, codes may not only refer to their members' behaviour. Individuals who are not members of professional bodies may well decide that it is appropriate to incorporate all or part of an 'official' code into their personal ethical standards.

There are several important reasons why professional codes of conduct exist. These include:

- To allow those inside and outside a profession – including members of the general public – to evaluate exactly what may be appropriately expected from members of that profession.
- To provide clear and *public* definitions of what is – and is not – viewed as acceptable professional behaviour.
- To allow the profession as a whole to support an individual who is maintaining an agreed viewpoint.

The expression of an 'official' view of professional behaviour has several very real advantages. First, setting out a detailed written code makes it much easier for individuals who are new to the field to understand and appreciate the range of circumstances that might be met in their professional lives. It is important to stress that such planning is not just concerned with uncommon problems. Some situations may be extremely familiar, but that need not mean they are consequently unimportant.

A comprehensive range of events and activities, well beyond the scope of even a very well-informed individual, may need to be anticipated for even an expert to feel professionally secure. The pressures of modern business and the barrage of day-to-day demands mean that it is all too easy to lose sight of the wider perspectives of professional work. The nature of specialization, too, is inherently likely to obscure the more extended implications of professional actions.

On an industry-wide scale, codes of conduct allow the greater weight of collective views to be felt. Publication by professional bodies means that the general public may be reassured that those working within a field are also concerned with its standards. Closer to home, individual commercial decisions by clients and customers can undoubtedly be enhanced by the confidence engendered through a well-publicized professional code.

Quite simply, this is analogous to the establishment of international software standards. Once established, proper compliance with such standards can be advertised and depended upon. Whoever actually supplies code, and wherever in the world they may be located, customers may then be sure of what they are buying.

In order to become a member of a professional society, an individual must normally demonstrate high standards of professional competence, or considerable experience, or both. Consequently, if (as an additional condition of membership) every rank and file member of a professional organization must subscribe to the same code of conduct, potential customers and employers may be certain, without further enquiry, of high standards in both skill and behaviour.

As mentioned earlier in this chapter, the collective expression of what is accepted as appropriate behaviour for members is at the core of a professional association. All members are able to contribute to the debate. Once rules are in place, however, it is important to emphasize that, even if it were otherwise quite legal, all behaviour defined by a professional body as inappropriate is not permitted.

Breaches of professional conduct are understandably taken seriously – penalties for ignoring professional codes may extend to actual expulsion. Any member of a profession, or at least those who wish to remain members, must therefore acknowledge constraints on their behaviour by accepting the limits of the relevant professional code.

Wider concepts

On a wider level , it would be worthwhile if all scientists were aware of the need for appropriate professional behaviour. Figure 7.1 reproduces a universal 'professional oath', proposed as a scientist's version of the traditional Hippocratic Oath of the medical profession. The London-based Institute for Social Inventions[2] has so far succeeded in obtaining the signatures of around twenty Nobel Laureates and a large number of other distinguished scientists, as well as obtaining support for the Oath from educational establishments throughout the world, including the Universities of Sussex and Surrey in the UK.

The concept of a professional oath for scientists, while certainly new, is an excellent one. There are obvious advantages in the concept, quite apart from the crucial individual commitment to good practice inherent in this document. For example, scientists generally have not always enjoyed a good public image. A formal oath, such as this one, being publicly taken at graduation would demonstrate a different view to both individual specialists and the general public.

Scientists should believe that their work is deserving of such attention. Professional practice overall might be improved if the Scientist's Oath became more widely accepted.

Hippocratic Oath for Scientists, Engineers and Executives

I vow to practise my profession with conscience and dignity;

I will strive to apply my skills only with the utmost respect for the well-being of humanity, the earth and all its species;

I will not permit considerations of nationality, politics, prejudice or material advancement to intervene between my work and this duty to present and future generations;

I make this Oath solemnly, freely and upon my honour.

Signed _____ Date_____

The signatories of this Oath include the following Nobel Laureates: Hannes Alven, J. Georg Bednorz, Sir John Cornforth, Prof. Jean Dausset, Manfred Eigen, Prof. Otto Fischer, William Fowler, Herbert Hauptman, Dudley Herschbach, Prof. Robert Huber, Brian Josephson, Prof. Klaus von Klitzing, Linus Pauling, Max Perutz, Heinrich Rohrer, Abdus Salam, Prof. Maurice Wilkins and Sir John Kendrew, President of the International Council of Scientific Unions. The Oath has also been signed by university Vice-Chancellors or equivalents including: Professor Gerald Fowler, Rector of the North East London Polytechnic, Professor Geoffrey Hall, Director of the Brighton Polytechnic, David Melville, Vice Rector, Lancashire Polytechnic, Sir Leslie Fielding, Vice-Chancellor, University of Sussex, and Professor Anthony Kelly, Vice-Chancellor of the University of Surrey; in the U.S.A. by Daniel Perlman, President of Suffolk University, Humphrey Tonkin, President, University of Hartford, John Slaughter, President, Occidental College, Stephen Sample, President, State University of New York at Buffalo, Paul Stabile, Associate Vice-President, Duquesne University, Owen Nichols, Vice-President, Howard University, Harold Proshansky, President of the Graduate School and University Center, City University of New York and Dr Jack Seilheimer, Dean of the College of Science and Mathematics at the University of Southern Colorado; in Australia by the Vice-Chancellor, University of Melbourne, Dr Herrman, Director, Footscray Institute of Technology, and Prof. Di Yerbury, Vice-Chancellor, Macquarie University; in New Zealand by R.F. Meyer, Dean of the School of Engineering, University of Auckland; in the Argentine by Dr Felix Cernuschi, Dean of the Faculty of Engineering, Universidad de Buenos Aires; in the Republic of China by Ta-Nien Yuan, President of the National Chiao Tung University. If you are willing to be added to the list of signatories, please keep this copy, but send your details to the publishers: *The Institute for Social Inventions*, 20 Heber Road, London NW2 6AA, UK, tel 081 208 2853, fax 081 452 6434.

Figure 7.1   Scientist's Oath

Personal vs. professional issues

Before moving on to examine the BCS Code of Practice in detail, it seems appropriate first to distinguish between two very different ways of responding to specialist professional issues. Traditionally, professionals have grouped together into professional bodies, which have then acted as arbiters of behaviour. In the UK, the BMA (British Medical

Association) and the Law Society are two longstanding examples. With changes in society and the advent of new technologies, many other hierarchical professional associations have been formed. However, there are alternatives to viewing professional practice as something to be fixed and regulated from above.

Richard Stallman, who was the inventor of the original EMACS editor, is an example of a personal attempt to define what should be considered appropriate professional behaviour for a software engineer. He wrote a complete, UNIX-compatible software system called GNU – standing for Gnu's Not UNIX[3] – with the intention of giving it away. He presented his philosophy in the aptly-named Gnu Manifesto,[4] which, although not updated since 1985, is still well worth reading. Here is an extract from the Manifesto, which sums up Stallman's philosophy:

> Many programmers are unhappy about the commercialization of system software. It may enable them to make more money, but it requires them to feel in conflict with other programmers in general rather than feel as comrades. The fundamental act of friendship among programmers is the sharing of programs; marketing arrangements now typically used essentially forbid programmers to treat others as friends. The purchaser of software must choose between friendship and obeying the law. Naturally, many decide that friendship is more important. But those who believe in law often do not feel at ease with either choice. They become cynical and think that programming is just a way of making money.
>
> By working on and using GNU rather than proprietary programs, we can be hospitable to everyone and obey the law. In addition, GNU serves as an example to inspire and a banner to rally others to join us in sharing.
>
> This can give us a feeling of harmony which is impossible if we use software that is not free. For about half the programmers I talk to, this is an important happiness that money cannot replace.

Although most of us may not be able or even wish to follow such individual ideas to their limits, knowledge of alternative views to those of the professional 'establishment' is important. Unquestioning acceptance, even of professional codes, is not recommended; so such alternative views should be considered, even if they may be ultimately discarded. Even the most convinced supporter of professionalism should surely have made an informed choice.

The BCS Code of Practice and Conduct

The British Computer Society (formally known as the Society of Information Systems Engineering; referred to here as the BCS) was established by Royal Charter in 1984, with the intention of representing professional computer scientists in the UK.

The BCS has always placed considerable importance on professional skills and responsibilities. After extensive consultation within and beyond the Information Systems field, in 1992 the Society's Professional Advisory Committee – consisting of experienced practitioners – recommended the BCS Council to adapt a new and comprehensive *BCS Code of Practice*. This official Code sets out the authoritative views of the BCS on all aspects of professional practice, and is binding upon BCS members.

As has been suggested above, a solid knowledge of the BCS Code is essential to any UK practitioner in the field of software engineering, whether or not they are or intend to be members of the BCS. The code is also of relevance outside the UK, although practitioners in the USA should certainly consider it in association with the ACM's *Code of Ethics and Professional Conduct*.

Although the BCS Code of Practice is the definitive document, the BCS pamphlet *British Computer Society Code of Conduct*[5] summarizes it, and is certainly more accessible.

The code of practice has a complex series of Level One (brief, defining) and Level Two (supportive rationale) statements. The pamphlet sets out the essentials of the BCS Code much more simply by grouping its central points under four main headings:

- The Public Interest
- Duty to Employers and Clients
- Duty to the Profession
- Professional Competence and Integrity

These headings accurately indicate the broad scale and wide scope of the code. Each of the four sections contains a number of specific points.[6]

By discussing points from each heading, it is possible to gather a reasonably detailed knowledge of the Code's provisions, and of the ways in which they might be interpreted. The following sections look at each of the four main headings in turn and place them in context.

The Public Interest[7]

In common with other professional organizations, the BCS understandably places considerable importance on protection of the public.

Members of the BCS should not only have knowledge and understanding of the relevant legislation and standards, but are expected to observe them. The rights of third parties must also be regarded and respected. However, the code additionally looks to wider issues. A central clause directly emphasizes the need for computer scientists to have regard for basic human rights; public health, safety, and concern for the environment are also addressed.

Such issues may not usually be at the forefront of a software engineer's mind. They are nevertheless of crucial importance. The designers of a computer system may, through their work, influence the lives of only a few individuals, or of many others, perhaps including people they have never met or even seen. All are important. The world we live in is made from the consequences of professional decisions; and it is perhaps too easy to leave for others consideration of the wider effects our work may have. 'It's not my responsibility. I'm just concerned with the software' is not an unusual response. However, our software and our systems *are* our responsibility; and, as I have stressed, we need to be aware of this even if we are not BCS members.

Duty to Employers and Clients

It is surely essential that clients should always be able to trust and rely on professional advice. Even those who do not believe that computing should be viewed as a 'profession' would undoubtedly accept that the advice of a computer specialist should be able to be relied upon.

What might this mean? For example, if clients pay a consultant to advise on the best commercial accounting system for their needs, they have a right to expect an objective response, not the automatic advice of a sales person, to buy a package from his or her company. It is only reasonable to expect that any professional will be in a position to advise client or customer objectively – individuals will not, for example, use the opportunity of a request for neutral advice to promote systems in which they have a financial interest.

Of course, occasions will arise when consultants objectively believe that their own product is indeed the best choice for a client. In this case, they must make a full disclosure of their involvement to the client *before* making their recommendation. The same action is essential, for example, where a commission is payable from a third party – the client needs to know of it before making a decision!

A similar approach is relevant when working within a company. An employer naturally expects a software engineer, for example, to perform work to an agreed standard. If, without agreement, an engineer instead applies an alternative, designed principally to increase the engineer's overtime pay, that person may be acting unethically.

Confidentiality is also important in a world where data held on computers may well be valuable, or sensitive, or both. For instance, it can easily happen, in the course of professional work, that a software engineer becomes aware of information which is confidential. This is not at all uncommon – it could easily be argued, for example, that the designer or maintainer of a database has much fuller access to it than any of its likely users.

The ability to access information, however, does not convey freedom to distribute it. The BCS Code makes it clear that information gained through professional duties should never be disclosed (unless by the consent of the client, or by Court order).

Another area of potential difficulty lies in making clients aware of the limitations of professional work, as well as its advantages. Of course, completion of work should ideally always be to time and within the budget. In real life, however, this condition may sometimes prove surprisingly difficult to achieve. Should a realistic assessment show that – for instance – an overrun is likely, the ethical software engineer should make the customer aware of the possibility in good time. Naturally, any possible consequences of the overrun need to be explained, too.

Summary

There is nothing dramatic or remarkable about the actions expected by the preceding section – common sense should indicate the appropriate ethical choice. After all, a software engineer who lies about deadlines, takes advantage of confidential information from clients and makes recommendations on the basis of personal profit is clearly not someone to employ.

Why, then, is it necessary to detail these points? It is not merely to make the ground rules clear, important as that is. It is also a good illustration of advantages which membership of organizations like the BCS can bring. We must work in a world where, unfortunately, unreliable computer scientists do exist. Making new customers and clients aware that you follow the BCS code could therefore be a sensible precaution.

Duty to the Profession

It is necessary to appreciate that belonging to a professional body does not simply involve taking from it what you need in the way of status and support. Membership brings responsibilities, too. The BCS expects that its members will seek to uphold its reputation, both passively, in avoiding actions which could bring it into disrepute, and actively, by working to positively improve the public image of the profession. Members are expected to be alert for false and misleading statements about their profession in order to counter them. Despite (or perhaps because of) the need to present a positive image of the profession, BCS members must not make any public statement in their professional capacity unless they are both properly qualified and authorized to do so.

It is certainly arguable that such responsibilities should also be carried by those outside the BCS – the computing profession as a whole. We all carry an obligation to ensure that our profession is well regarded, and, of course, we all stand to benefit if it is.

Professional Competence and Integrity

The final section of the BCS code addresses the tricky area of professional competence.

A key point to establish here is that membership of a professional body is never the end of a development process. To obtain membership, and then take no further efforts – particularly to upgrade relevant knowledge – is, quite understandably, held to be insufficient. In a fast-moving field, such as computing, it is essential to keep in touch with both technological developments and altering standards. To do this is not just reassuring to clients, but of real importance in personal and professional development.

Self-knowledge, of your own individual abilities and competence, is also important. Naturally, you must be aware of what you are able to accomplish professionally. Just as important, though, is to understand and appreciate what you *cannot* do. Despite obvious short-term advantages, it is both unethical and unprofessional to accept work for which you are not qualified. Any professional opinion you give, for example, should be not just objective, but well founded.

Final points in this section of the BCS code cover more general aspects of 'professional' behaviour, common to most professions – not dropping a contract without proper notice, avoiding conflicts of interest, working to good, accepted standards and encouraging subordinates to do so too. It is important to appreciate that these generally expected standards of 'professional' behaviour, common to other professions, are as much part of the code as standards which are unique to computer science.

Conclusions

If individuals are to build an effective ethical code, they must draw upon a range of ideas and experiences. The BCS code has the advantage of bringing together a large number of the ethical issues which will confront anyone in professional practice as a computer scientist. It also presents guidelines, and responses to them, which are widely held to be appropriate. Of course, membership of the BCS automatically (and properly) brings with it a commitment to honour all points in the code.

Important as the points covered in it are, I do not suggest that this – or any – code should ever be followed unthinkingly, or incorporated into a personal set of beliefs without question. Codes are not set in stone, and should never be thought of as a substitute for individual thought. In this case, the profession as well as the individual is developing, and it is important that the code is kept under review. BCS members have a responsibility to help in its evolution.

Questions

1. Have you ever seen a professional code (not necessarily a computing code)? If so, what do you remember about it?
2. What do you consider should be the most important points to put into a code of computing?
3. How might the professional codes of different countries vary? What reasons might there be for this?
4. What do you feel a UK code of computing might have in common with the codes of other professions?
5. Which of the points listed in Appendix E do you consider are the *most* important? Why?
6. Which of the points listed in Appendix E do you consider are the *least* important? Why?

Notes

[1] Although they share the professional approach described in this chapter, the IAP (Institution of Analysts and Programmers) currently has no professional Code. Appendix D details their views.

[2] The Institute for Social Inventions, 20 Heber Road, London NW2 6AA; telephone 0181 208 2853.

[3] The acronym is, of course, deliberately recursive.

[4] Available by anonymous ftp from `labrea.stanford.edu` in the directory `/pub/gnu/GNUinfo` or from `svin02.info.win.tue.nl` in the directory `/pub/gnu/GNUinfo`.

[5] Together with an official summary of the ACM Code, the BCS Code of Conduct is reproduced in Appendix E.

[6] It is available by post from the BCS.

[7] In contrast to the more detailed BCS document, the ACM Code (also reproduced in Appendix Five) is divided into general headings only, although it covers much the same ground. The area of 'public interest' is described there under 'General Moral Imperatives'.

8

Systems management and 'hacking'

Super user vs. informal user? Systems management, the professional maintenance of a networked computer system, and 'hacking' – unofficial interaction with computer systems – may be at different ends of a wide spectrum, but there are ethical issues which are relevant to both. This chapter looks at the responsibilities involved in developing and maintaining a computer system, and discusses the ethics of unauthorized access. It concludes with an examination of viruses and software theft.

Systems management

Systems administrators are expected to ensure that their computer systems run smoothly and efficiently, and that data stored on them is safe and secure from both loss and unauthorized access.

What does this mean in practice?

Well, a typical user definition of a well-run system is one where systems administration is actually invisible – machines appear to run themselves, seamlessly and efficiently. For this reason, users may be unaware that the task of systems administration is far from easy.

Users may also not appreciate that, in order to do their job properly, administrators have to be allowed sweeping powers over a computer system. Indeed, the power of a system administrator, as 'super user', over their machine is virtually infinite: they can access any data passing through their machine, can monitor, create and destroy files, and, in particular, they automatically have the power to electronically 'become' any of their users, and are then able to behave as if that person's data were their own.

If all power corrupts, then, in the light of these awesome powers, it seems encouraging that systems administrators as a class generally seem to be aware and responsible people. Most are aware of the need to police themselves, since naturally even the most skilled user could not do so. However, power and responsibility do not always go together. It is clearly very important that guidelines for designing and maintaining computer systems are made clear to everyone – including, of course, their users. The principal alternative, leaving policy to *ad hoc* development by different administrators and managers, has clear and obvious disadvantages.

As an example of what can happen, consider a list of questions put to one system administrator. His site had offered an anonymous access point to a special Internet newsgroup for the survivors of sexual abuse. (ASAR, or, more properly, `alt.sexual.abuse.recovery`). Some abuse survivors understandably prefer anonymity, yet might nevertheless benefit by drawing support from others with similar experiences. One answer is to post mail through a special system, which maintains a register of identification details but forwards messages to newsgroups or individuals only after removing personal identification.

In this case, the person responsible for administering the system appears to have caused concern over behaviour which was widely perceived as inappropriate. The following questions, directed in an open letter[1] to the system administrator, are taken from a longer posting:

> Is it your responsibility, as a system administrator, (particularly on an ASARian system where privacy is so emphasized and needed) to plug the potential holes in your system that may lead to a violation of privacy?
>
> Is it your responsibility, as a system administrator, to not abuse the same holes (if/when found) as a user or as a super user on the system until they are plugged?
>
> Do you consider yourself to be a system administrator when you are logged on as a super user?
>
> Do you consider yourself to be a system administrator when you are logged on as a user?
>
> Do you consider yourself to be a system administrator when you are not logged on to [name of anonymous system]?
>
> Is it your responsibility, as a system administrator *AND* as a user of [name of anonymous system], to not breach user's privacy by accessing their files, or doing any other activity that would breach their privacy with, or without, their knowing of said actions?

These are serious questions, which go to the heart of the responsibilities of an administrator. Their implications should be considered carefully.

Although little or no attention is normally given to the ethics of system management, I suggest that these questions indicate that anyone who takes responsibility for maintaining a computer network needs to be quite clear about what is expected of them ethically, as well as practically. It is usually true that, during the appointment of systems administration staff, most attention is understandably given to clarifying practical responsibilities. However, in order for candidates to know whether they wish to take the job, there is just as much need to discuss the less easily defined ethical expectations.

> Dave was employed as a computer specialist by a medium-sized company, principally to support their network and electronic mail. It became clear that the Technical Director, who had originally set up the mail system, maintained a log of all email messages, and made copies of all private mail of interest to him. Dave learned that he was expected to continue monitoring mail (although, interestingly, was told not to actually read it himself), and to pass on copies of mail from and to selected employees.

The point here is not that such action is automatically unethical; that must depend upon individual circumstances. The data was generated by employees in the course of their work, so, legally, the Technical Director is probably in the clear.

There are, however, two ethical points which certainly are at issue. The first is whether the concerned employees *know* that their mail may be monitored and copied. If they do not, then the action is, almost certainly, unethical, and Dave would be quite justified in feeling unhappy about the practice.

The second point concerns Dave himself. While he is expected to continue a policy he may personally find unethical, he was never given an opportunity to evaluate whether or not he wished to undertake this role. If he found it distasteful, Dave's only choice would be to leave the job or to persuade the Technical Director to change his policy.

In these circumstances, the onus was clearly on the director to have made clear his expectations at an earlier stage, while Dave could still draw back from the job application. That he did not do so may have reflected the director's own ambivalent feelings about the monitoring. However, employers have a responsibility to inform new staff fully about the whole range of their work. To concentrate purely on practical issues is understandable, but should be resisted.

One way of resolving the problems of hidden assumptions is for company and group philosophy to be something which is discussed openly, and to be generally known and accepted. Then, when there is a need to employ a new member of staff, it is possible to give candidates an accurate and detailed impression of what working in that setting will involve. Of course, existing workers are likely to benefit from this policy, too.

A need for full discussion of a post's responsibilities is, of course, relevant to all types of employment with computers, and not simply work in systems administration.

When specifically considering the responsibilities of a systems administrator, it is probably sufficient to clarify general rules and expectations, rather than attempting to develop a lengthy specific contract. However, there is clearly a need for any administrator to understand what is, and what is not, permitted by the organization. Of course, systems administrators need first to consider what they personally feel is appropriate and inappropriate in professional behaviour.

It is also essential that users of the computer system are made equally aware of these issues, and understand the views of organization and administrator.

The enormous differences between various commercial, business and professional computer users make it impossible to give specific recommendations here. Some companies view any data or information generated by their employees in company time or on company equipment as automatically belonging to the company. In contrast, most universities tend to consider a user's files to be their personal property.

Responsibility does, of course, work both ways.

Joe is a self-confessed 'free spirit', who had a series of computing jobs in and around San Francisco. He prided himself on always doing good work for his various employers, but, whenever possible, made a habit of opening up any system he worked on, to allow him to gain access to it in the future. Sometimes he passed on access information to friends. Joe viewed himself as a liberator, setting free computers from their boring business owners.

Was Joe acting ethically? Even if he was authorized to work on a system, his employers had certainly not anticipated that he would use this super user authority to undermine their system security. Concern is certainly justified. As will be discussed later in this chapter, users who have not been authorized to enter a computer system can cause considerable problems. It was unclear exactly why Joe himself wanted to be able to revisit systems on which he had worked in the past; but his desire to do so was not necessarily unethical. The relevant point, though, is not that he was entering the system, but that he was entering the system without the knowledge or permission of the current systems administrator. He was able to do this only because he had previously concealed his 'open system' philosophy, and he had misused access provided through a contract which had paid him for system support.

It is therefore probably fair to suggest that Joe was acting unethically, both in allowing unauthorized users to have access to systems and in himself obtaining access after his reasons for doing so were over. Ironically, had he been open about his actions his behaviour would probably not have been unethical; but then, of course, it is unlikely that he would have been employed in a position which allowed him such powers.

Inevitably, there are also sometimes problems between administrators and managers. Typically, a manager might propose new policies which have unplanned and unexpected implications for the management of a computer system. Or a new technical development may become available which someone in authority feels should be implemented immediately. In these circumstances, when changes are proposed without sufficient input from the administrator, it is particularly important for the administrator to consider the implications, and speak out if necessary. All concerned (ideally including representative users) should then take time to consider any implications of the changes – together with, of course, ethical implications.

Although managers should have initiated such a discussion earlier, it is not solely their responsibility to consider ethical issues. Everyone involved has a legitimate concern. If those responsible for organizing ethical discussions do not do so, the issues should not therefore be ignored. Indeed, as the people responsible for 'their' systems, administrators should be in the front line in identifying potential risk.

This makes good sense – it is the systems administrators who will, inevitably, be associated with changes to their machines, and they who must deal with the consequences. Similarly, because even simple changes may have unanticipated results, the implementation of internal changes to the way systems operate should include a consideration of any possible ethical repercussions. Systems administrators are not just concerned with hardware and software, however much they may wish they were.

> Marcel was responsible for an office computer system with over fifty users. After he had requested the purchase of additional disk capacity, management decided to impose a policy of stricter disk quotas. The plan was for a sliding scale, where senior managers (who needed space least) had the largest disk quotas, while junior staff would have virtually no quota. Although not anxious to upset his boss, Marcel felt the policy unreasonable and refused to implement it. A full discussion followed, but the debate was soon cut short by purchase of new disks. The variable quota policy was allowed to lapse.

Whatever the particular philosophy of the organization, there should be informed awareness on the part of employer, systems administrator and system users of local rules and expectations. Changes should be carefully considered, and those involved should be continually aware of the need to consider ethical implications. Workers, too, should be prepared to be open about their ethical standards and beliefs, and especially what they consider is appropriate conduct. A need for ethical behaviour is seldom one-sided.

Bulletin boards

Although they are normally operated by volunteers or enthusiasts (often using their own equipment) the responsibilities involved in running bulletin boards (or BBS) are in many ways very similar to those faced by system administrators. (Incidentally, although many BBS have a connection to the Internet, Internet postings themselves are discussed in the next chapter.)

A BBS is often run from a microcomputer, supported by a large hard disk, and connected to a modem. Users dial the BBS number, and after connection are then able to up- and download files, read information and post messages to each other. The systems operator, or 'sysop', maintains the system, and sometimes charges users a fee for doing so.

Mail sent through such a BBS may feel to a user as though it is private, but as a super user the sysop can readily access and read all the email passing through the board.

Some years ago, when accessing a BBS from home via a computer and modem, Tony discovered that the sysop of a large UK specialist board he regularly used apparently had an established practice of monitoring private mail. Any message, however personal, which was stored on his board might be read. The sysop actually quoted a section of a private email message he had copied, and, when challenged, was quite surprised his behaviour had caused offence.

Again, it is not *necessarily* unethical for someone to act in this way. What is unethical is to do so secretly, and, in particular, to allow users of a system to believe they are communicating privately and in confidence when they are not.

As discussed in Chapter 9 in relation to Internet newsgroups, there are additional legal problems facing those sites acting as news relays. These legal concerns are also of interest to those operating BBS, particularly specialist boards which may attract callers from a wide area. Recent developments in the US suggest that to allow downloading of material which is legal in the home state of a BBS, may still place the BBS at risk of prosecution if a call is made to it from a state with more restrictive legislation. For example, if a BBS in Los Angeles is accessed from outside California, and material illegal under *that* state's law is downloaded, a crime may have been committed.

There is widespread public concern over the use of computer networks to distribute 'unauthorized' material. Much of this concern may be founded upon misconceptions, and involve concepts which, to a computer professional, may seem absurd. For example, the London *Times* of 16 June 1994, said (on page 2)

> … Children as young as five have access to the material, which features real sex acts, through educational CD-ROM discs that have been corrupted via electronic mail and computer clubs…

The computer application which was apparently able to corrupt and alter a CD-ROM was unfortunately not specified.

In the UK, it is illegal to download or electronically distribute sexually oriented material which may be perfectly legal, and freely available, in most other European countries. This is of considerable concern to those involved in BBS, because almost all boards allow users to upload files likely to be of interest to others, and provide an area where this may be done. The operator of a UK board must therefore be constantly on guard against the uploading to their BBS of potentially illegal material obtained from outside the UK. (As discussed later, 'hacking' information is sometimes posted to specialist BBS in a similar way.)

Some legislators take the issue very seriously. Emma Nicholson is a Conservative MP who has taken a continuing interest in the regulation of computing. Writing in the June 1994 issue of *Government Computing*, she proposed the licensing of all UK bulletin boards under a 'carefully chosen' set of standards, and continued:

> ... Random checks could be made ensuring that these standards were being maintained, and failure to do so would result in the withdrawal of the license, punitive fines, confiscation of equipment and disconnection.
>
> It should be made illegal to contact unlicensed bulletin boards and any attempt to do so might also result in punitive fines, confiscation of equipment and disconnection. The punishment should be applied to both the user and the owner of the equipment used unless it can be proved that the owner has taken all reasonable steps to secure against misuse.

However impractical such suggestions may appear to those with technical knowledge – after all, despite all attempts at suppression, pirate radio is still with us – there is no doubt that the growing desire of individuals to communicate electronically has resulted in a perceived risk to sections of society. Consider the ease with which a schoolchild may obtain a lurid magazine, and compare the cost and difficulty of obtaining the same pictures in electronic form; and reflect on the differing responses of politicians and the popular press to the corner newsagent and the existence of a BBS with suspect material.

Are existing laws on publishing to be applied to electronic media because allowing material to be downloaded is really 'publishing' it? Many BBS throughout the world are connected to the Internet; consequently, many articles are not locally generated. If distributing such postings is to be construed as 'publishing' them, then any news site or BBS in the UK is already at risk of being sued over material the operators not only knew nothing about, but which, realistically, they could not.

This is not to discount the fact that there is undoubtedly a need for some accepted view which defines the position of the electronic media. Uniformity of policy and action between different countries, even though such action may be very difficult to coordinate, would clearly be sensible. This issue is discussed as part of the airing of issues surrounding use of electronic mail, in Chapter 9.

So far in this chapter, we have looked at the role of a system administrator, the person responsible for the smooth running of a system and the protection of data stored on it, and the similar responsibilities of the sysop of a BBS. Although the 'super user' powers of administrators are great, they should be used with caution, and certainly with responsibility. Although it is probably impossible to impose clear rules,[2] administrators nevertheless need to be aware not only of their employer's expectations, but of their own beliefs and views, too.

It is very important for administrators to take these issues seriously. Ordinary system users may understandably depend upon the security and safety of 'their' system, and never think about what is going on behind the scenes.

Unofficial access

'Hacking' is now an emotive term. Originally, back in the 1960s and 1970s, it was used to describe someone working with computers who was particularly technically knowledgeable. Then there was no implication that someone known as a computer 'hacker' would act illegally; indeed, the early hackers took the position seriously enough to establish their own ethical code, known as the Hacker Ethic.[3] Although both the social and the computing environment have greatly changed since it was written, the creation of the Ethic was sincere, as were its intentions. There were five principal values comprising the early Hacker Ethic:

- Access to computers – and anything which might teach you something about the way the world works – should be unlimited and total. Always yield to the Hands-On Imperative!
- All information should be free.
- Mistrust Authority – Promote Decentralization.
- Hackers should be judged by their hacking, not bogus criteria such as degrees, age, race or position.
- You can create art and beauty on a computer.

The focus of the Hacker Ethic is, perhaps understandably in the circumstances, on the hacker. Among the areas left out are the rights of users and consideration of a computer scientist's responsibilities to them.

Some solid citizens, long established in computer science, may still nostalgically think of themselves as hackers. However, as tends to happen with language, the use of the term 'hacker' expanded and its definition broadened. Today, despite historical claims, my definition of hacking is: 'obtaining and exploiting unofficial access to a computer system'. This may be more topical. The currently accepted view of a hacker is therefore someone who uses a specialized knowledge of computer systems to obtain illegal access to them. Probably, too, once they have obtained access to a system, a hacker would be expected to steal and corrupt data.

Typical actions taken by hackers include breaking into public and private databases, sometimes just to see if it is possible, sometimes for more serious reasons, such as altering marks in a school computer or altering a credit rating. Information on how to accomplish these and other tasks is sometimes posted – anonymously, of course – to specialist bulletin boards. Serious hackers may use a succession of computers as staging posts, to route a continuing series of attacks on different systems. The book *Cuckoo's Egg*, by Clifford Stohl describes how military computers in the USA were attacked by hackers in Germany through a whole series of such staging posts. It is obviously much more difficult to trace an attack made in this way to its source.

Computer viruses

Some individuals, often describing themselves as 'hackers', anonymously release destructive software known (because of both the manner and ease with which they spread) as computer 'viruses'. These applications spread from machine to machine via disk or network links, and are not normally visible to a user. A virus may be 'benign', in which case it is intended to do nothing but reproduce itself, and perhaps display a message. Its counterpart is 'destructive', when behaviour is designed to destroy data and wreck systems. Even a virus intended as 'benign' may, however, be dangerous; modifying a computer system in any way without the knowledge of the owner can create potential problems.

I do not know of any ethical defence for creating or deliberately circulating a virus application.

Is there an ethical position on hacking?

It is certainly unrealistic to expect everyone to appreciate automatically the validity of global ethical rules. As we have argued before, simply because ethical views are individual, it is not often possible to make absolute statements. As a simple illustration of this point, consider this proposal: if there is one rule which most people would accept to have universal justification, it is probably a variation of 'thou shalt not kill'. Yet anyone entering any of the armed services will rapidly be given a different perspective. Medals are awarded for killing an approved enemy.

If even a basic, obvious ethical point with wide social acceptance may be modified by other pressures, where does this leave hacking? Given the broad range of different views, is it possible to create a generally acceptable ethical attitude?

There are two different positions to consider.

First, if computers are viewed as material possessions, then electronic entry to a computer system can be looked on as very similar to physical entry into an office or home. Unless there is a specific invitation, or previous permission to enter, this is trespass, if not unlawful entry. Hackers have a typical defence, though: they are entering to 'test for loopholes in the software'. Is this realistic? If challenged, many hackers claim to know a 'friend of a friend', who was paid by a large company to test its computer systems for security loopholes. This is, of course, comparable to paying a burglar to attack your home in the hope that the burglar may reveal security weaknesses.

I once lived in a remote rural setting, where keys left in a car would still be untouched after a week, and where everyone really did leave doors unlocked. Even if they had explained that households should be grateful for security checking, an individual who went around the neighbourhood opening those unlocked doors and exploring inside people's houses would not have been welcome. Let me pursue the analogy further. What would most people think of someone who broke into your home and went through your desk, reading whatever letters and personal material they happened to find? On the face of it, there seems, so far, to be a clear legal and ethical case against hacking into someone else's computer system.

However, there is a second position. This follows the contention that computers are not to be viewed as material possessions, belonging to one business, or another. There is, the view runs, an undefined global community of computing, where the physical ownership of each machine is secondary to the benefit to its users. Sometimes, taking the Internet as a limited example, supporters claim that exploring this electronic world is somehow above such considerations as 'yours' and 'mine'

– electrons belong to no one. If there is a cost, big business can afford to pay it.

This fairly anarchic philosophy really needs to be discussed in detail to be fully appreciated. There are clear strengths to the idea, particularly in view of the advantages of openness. The general enrichment which tends to come from wide information distribution may mean developers never have to 'reinvent the wheel', or needlessly design from scratch something which already exists elsewhere. However, the fairly crucial question of cost – who actually pays for this, and why they should – is generally overlooked. It might be thought that all the existing 'users' really need to be consulted before their systems are opened to wider exploration, too.

Of course individuals must decide for themselves whether the idea of 'hacking' is appropriate for their beliefs and circumstances. Nevertheless, it does seem that the concept, as currently defined, is difficult to justify ethically.

Software theft

Another area of conflict between different ethical values is the unauthorized use of computer software. This is known as either 'bootleg' or 'pirated' software, by its supporters, or as 'illegal' or 'stolen' software, by software producers. Copying and distribution of such software is perceived as a real threat, especially by those writing and selling commercial programs for microcomputers. Enormous sums in sales are believed to be lost by the use of illegally copied programs; but it is also claimed that the chances of illegal users ever buying original copies of the software were always vanishingly small.

Stealing may be morally wrong, but, if software suppliers are to be believed, most of us have used bootleg software at one time or another. Possibly because of the physical and emotional distance of the application from its real owner, to most users copying software seldom appears to feel like *stealing*. People who would never dream of shoplifting are prepared to casually borrow and duplicate copyright disks and to photocopy manuals. The practice is widespread – it is probably a rare personal hard disk which has absolutely no illegal software on it (mine is the exception, of course). Many commercial users, too, have their share of illegal microcomputer software, although copying of mainframe packages, perhaps because of their complexity, is seen as far less of a problem.

The easy stand to make here is to declare all use of unauthorized software to be unethical – and there is certainly a good case for doing so. The time and trouble involved in producing software – especially good software – is far greater than the average user may appreciate. To take the fruits of this work, and to pay nothing for it, seems clearly wrong.

However, the issue is complicated by the attitude of software vendors. Software is still largely seen as overpriced, perhaps because the sale price does not always bear an obvious relationship to development costs. The make of your machine, too, will probably affect the cost of software – a Macintosh user may have to pay more than the user of a PC, because, generally, Macintosh users are perceived as able to afford more. The situation is additionally complicated by the escalating costs of software: some commercial packages for personal computers cost up to a thousand pounds.

If buying a single package involves such high expenditure, users may understandably want to sample it first. Small groups of users may justify clubbing together to buy a single copy of software in order to copy it between them. 'At least', they claim, 'this makes one sale for the company; none of us could otherwise afford it'.

There is also a curious combination of status and simplicity involved in using unauthorized software. The risk of being caught is low, but there is still a sense of challenge; and, of course, it is easier and cheaper to use a program from a friend, rather than trudging down to a computer supplier to buy your own.

Software may therefore be 'pirated' because it is seen as unnecessarily expensive, hard to evaluate, more troublesome to buy, and, perhaps, because to do so is seen as challenging. Using such software certainly lowers the cost of personal computing, and there is little realistic risk of being caught.

However, this does not make the use of bootleg software ethical. An ethical position on copied programs is not influenced by the ease or difficulty in obtaining such software, or whether pirating a disk saves money. As always, it is very important for individuals to think through their views, remembering that ethical standards are not to be assumed and discarded casually. If an action is unethical, it is unethical. Whatever decision on the issue you reach, make sure that you have reached it with your eyes open, and are aware of both the immediate consequences, and the wider implications, both in terms of legality and ethics – and more pragmatic issues, too. If developers do not make a profit, they can no longer develop software, and the consequences may be unwelcome.

> David bought a personal computer called a Dragon (it was made in Wales). He made a habit of never buying software, but, instead, was always trying to swap disks with other owners.
>
> Little software was developed especially for the Dragon, and the manufacturer ceased production. There were of course other problems – but perhaps too many others behaved like David. His Dragon computer has for some years now lived in the bottom of a wardrobe. David, given the chance, will still grumble at length about computers and computer companies, and his bad investment.

The increasing use of new technology means there may be one possible answer to this issue. If users wish to try software before buying, suppliers are beginning to allow this, by publishing 'test' versions of software on CD-ROM, along with locked versions of the full program. A user may work with a limited version of a package – typically, the version supplied will not print or save data. If they like it, they can then contact the supplier, and on payment obtain from them a code number. This number then permits copying of a full version from the CD. A manual follows in due course, by post.

For the continued production of good quality software, there needs to be confidence on the part of software authors and distributors that their work will be adequately rewarded. While there are many pragmatic arguments for the illegal use of commercial software, this reality lies behind them all.

I would urge you finally to consider two issues as particularly important. First, 'shareware' – software developed by individuals and charged at very low rates. Production of shareware is almost invariably at a loss, and the software author needs all possible encouragement simply to stay developing and writing. Consider as a priority making certain that any shareware you use is always paid for. Secondly, of course discuss your ideas and views freely. Nevertheless, even those who are themselves prepared to use illegal software should think very carefully before encouraging others to do so.

Conclusions

This chapter has looked at the responsibilities of those professionally maintaining computer systems, and, on a smaller scale, those looking after bulletin boards. I have suggested an open approach and the involvement of all users of a system in the decisions made about its operation.

After a brief discussion of computer 'hacking', the chapter concluded with a look at the ethics of 'bootleg' software.

Questions

1. Systems administrators obviously have a responsibility to maintain their computer; but to whom *are* they responsible? Management? The users? Themselves?
2. There is a long history of protecting people from information they ought not to possess. Do you think there is information the users of a system ought not to have? Who should decide what it is, and on what grounds?
3. Where may a 'company philosophy' come from? Who might be responsible for formulating the philosophy of an organization towards its computer systems? What role could – and should – be played by computer staff?
4. Does the operator of a private BBS have any responsibility to the users of their board? If so, what might it be? If not, why not?
5. Perhaps the best way to understand arguments against hacking is to turn the case around, and to ask how you might feel if someone invaded your own computer system. What reasons might you put forward to justify keeping your computer and its files private? Would you be justified?
6. What might make an act of 'hacking' ethical?
7. What would your response be to someone attempting to hack into a system for which you were responsible? Think through your reasons for this response.
8. Do you possess any commercial software for which you have not paid? If so, why? Would you do this again?

Notes

[1] Although this posting was public, in view of the special sensitivity of the ASAR newsgroup specific permission was obtained before reproducing it here.
[2] For example, it would seem reasonable to forbid superusers having access to a user's files – but what if a user appears to be storing and distributing pornography? Or programs obtained illegally?
[3] Included in *Hackers – Heroes of the Computer Revolution*, Steven Levy, Anchor Press/ Doubleday, 1984.

9

Email and newsgroups

Distribution of personally generated information is a major task of most computer systems. Sometimes the information is communicated directly between individuals; sometimes it is intended for a wider audience. This chapter examines the way in which such data is distributed, and identifies points of potential ethical conflict in both personal electronic mail – email – and the wider distributions of Internet newsgroups. It includes some suggested guidelines.

What is email?

Email (electronic mail) may be viewed as a communications medium which forms a combination of conventional letter and telephone – with perhaps just a dash of fax, too. As the potential equivalent of all three, it has most of their advantages and problems, with the addition of some which are all its own.

An electronic message generated on one computer is transmitted to another, situated on the next desk or the next continent. To employ email, a user needs a computer connected to a network with suitable software. Normally, a person sending email types a letter, which may possibly include other computer files as 'enclosures'. When finished, it is 'posted' (via a networked mail system) to the recipient's email address. A networked mail system may be 'closed', in which case only local email addresses, or addresses within that organization, are valid. However, many local networks may have additional connections to other networks, often including the Internet. In this case, an electronic message may literally be sent to any suitable electronic address anywhere in the world, with actions as simple as sending a message to the next office.

There are considerable advantages to communication through email. It is very easily copied and distributed, may be readily stored and recalled, and, once equipment is in place, is extremely inexpensive to use. Electronic messages travel faster and are inherently cheaper than paper based ones, which are, of course, known to electronic communicators as 'snail-mail'.

Although a telephone call may potentially be faster, this is only true if a desired speaker can be immediately located. In contrast, there is no such difficulty with email – electronic messages may be sent 24 hours a day, and may be read by their addressees whenever they wish.

In view of these facts, it is understandable that electronic messaging systems and messages are rapidly becoming indispensable, not only to modern business organizations and higher education, but to an increasing number of private individuals, too.

Newsgroups

Not all electronic mail is directed from one person to another. Often, what is needed is a more general response; sometimes the identity of an individual able to help with a problem is unknown. In these and other cases, a user may, instead of posting an email message to a specific person, instead address their message to a 'newsgroup'. Newsgroups are similar to notice-boards, where postings' subjects may either be new or relate to other messages. Some popular groups generate an enormous volume of daily postings, and there are, literally, thousands of such groups, dealing with every aspect of human activity. Although many computer networks also have their own local newsgroups, most are available through the Internet, the global linking of computer systems.

An Internet newsgroup may be 'moderated', or 'open'. Moderated groups have lower traffic, and each displayed posting is vetted by the group's moderator for suitability. An open, or unmoderated, group is the nearest thing on earth to total free speech – anyone may post anything there, and, once sent, their email will be automatically distributed and read throughout the world. To make the system workable, an unwritten agreement between users restricts postings on specific subjects to relevant newsgroups. This rule is sometimes broken, but the vast range of available groups means that most people can readily find congenial company.

Sadly, despite its obvious advantages, there are a number of potential difficulties and ethical problems involved in the use of electronic communications. They may be divided into two groups: difficulties which follow ordinary use of the medium, and those involving malicious activities.

Issues in normal use of electronic communication

The first group of problems principally covers unexpected responses from others, which are sometimes a consequence of email. This often results from the unthinking employment of familiar working methods, which, although they may have worked well in a paper based environment, do not transfer appropriately to a more modern medium of communication.

Many new users have problems in understanding exactly how to classify an electronic message mentally. Is it, for example, to be considered as similar to a paper memo? There are certainly similarities, but to generate a typed inter-office memo involves several stages, at each of which the author may modify the text, or even decide to scrap the whole idea. This drawn-out process does not fit the generation of an electronic message, which, in contrast, is very quick and easy to produce. Far from spending time in considering what to write, many people create and send email spontaneously, often without pausing to consider their use of tone and language, or even if the message is really appropriate or necessary. (The actual content of email is discussed in more detail later in this section.)

A 'dash off a note and send it' attitude is understandable, because, unlike paper communications, email appears as transitory. A message can flash across a screen before seeming to vanish into electronic limbo. Indeed, with a keystroke or two, it may permanently disappear; copies of electronic messages do not need shredding. It is, though, a serious mistake to think of email as temporary. Although email messages can certainly be impermanent, the opposite is also true. Once sent, a copy of an unguarded personal message may easily be stored by a recipient for years, before, in the memorable phrase of one businessman, 'It comes back to haunt you'. For example:

```
... you should stand up to him! If *I* had
the [sales desk] you can be sure old
[Jones] would get told what to do with his
policy!
```

Because the messages shown on your screen and stored on your disk have gone, it does not mean that identical copies are not still available somewhere else, and they may remain available indefinitely. A message can, of course, also be printed out; a casual electronic jotting may in this way instantly and unexpectedly achieve the formal authority of a typed memo.

Apart from its primary task of conveying information to the addressee, what use may be made of your email? A posting to the Internet newsgroup `soc.culture.scientists` pointed out some specific problems:

> I wish to raise the question of the confidentiality of e-mail messages. This is provoked by a recent discussion with a colleague who feels free to broadcast in any way he sees fit e-mail (and, for that matter, hard mail) received from others. He recently sent me via e-mail all of the correspondence he has received in recent months.
>
> When I called him on the inappropriateness of this he responded that he does not believe in confidences. He says if something cannot be said openly do not say it. This is a very noble view, but it seems to me that as a matter of courtesy one should obtain permission from the author of a message before passing it on. Do I have any support in my view?

In the general discussion which followed, wide support was given to the concept of confidentiality in email communication. It may be, though, that the anonymous colleague actually has a case. Perhaps his own ethical code justifies him in believing that if something cannot be said openly, it should not be said. Even if you disagree with his view, there is surely a clear ethical case to be made for this approach.

However, where we must part ethical company with him is in the appropriateness of taking such action without first informing others. If, knowing you may publish my letter, I write to you anyway, my position is clear, and there is no room for complaint. In contrast, if I write with the expectation of privacy, and without my permission you publish the correspondence, your action is likely to be unethical.

There are further dangers, too. Leaving the issue of newsgroups aside for a moment, consider the ease with which a message may be diffused. For example, a personal message, sent by one individual, may be readily distributed to many others. Adding extra electronic addresses to the 'cc' (carbon copy) field of an email posting allows the number of recipients of an original message to be effortlessly increased. Postings to a local 'mailing group' can do such forwarding automatically; a single message to a group is distributed to every group member.

Additionally, because email is so easily duplicated, once received a message may also be copied and further distributed, with or without the knowledge of the original sender. This means that the eventual readership of a message may be much wider than was originally intended by the author. Is this important? It may well be. What you might be prepared to admit in private conversation or correspondence, you may understandably be reluctant to say in public – and, of course, electronic text can be very public indeed.

> The development manager of a software company responded to a
> helpful bug report from a user by sending a rather frank appraisal of
> the software, which, he felt, had been released too soon. The
> message was circulated widely, with unfortunate results.

There are in practice no laws which prevent such actions. Although conventions of behaviour have evolved in the 'electronic community' which make distribution of personal electronic mail in this way generally unacceptable, a user would be very unwise indeed to rely on them.

The likelihood of such problems is of course greatly increased once a posting is made to a public newsgroup – largely because there is literally no way to restrict distribution of a message once it has been publicly posted. Even if a message is subsequently 'killed' by its originator, copies will still be forwarded around the net, until the delete request catches up with the original message. Moreover, if the delete request has the same propagation as the original, who is to say that every site will obey them? Faked kill (delete) requests have been used to hassle people on the net – by automated software which generates a kill instruction to delete every article the victim posts. For this reason, some Internet sites normally disable kill processing. Of course, the delete message might even over-take the actual article in a queue somewhere, and subsequently be ig-nored, because the article to which it refers does not yet appear to exist. When the delayed article arrived, of course, it would then continue to be propagated as normal. However, even if delete requests were always obeyed and could never be faked, nothing can be done about people who have already read the message, and/or saved it to their own per-sonal filestore.

Given the additional ease with which a message sent to one specialist forum may be copied to others, it is clearly essential that newsgroup postings are not made without careful thought. As a contributor to the Internet newsgroup uk.misc put it:

> Anyway, one of the first rules of Usenet is to look around and see what is going on
> before putting your foot in it. The same basic principle is found in other aspects of life
> so why should the net be any different?

To summarize: email messages possess many advantages, and the use of electronic mail is certain to continue expanding. However, there are also problems involved in using the medium, particularly relating to the freedom with which electronic text may be duplicated and distributed. Posting to a newsgroup brings the considerable advantages of addressing a specialist readership, but an ill-considered posting still risks (however inadvertently) your appearing to act in a way seen as inappropriate. Once made, such a posting cannot be satisfactorily removed.

Posting to a newsgroup makes it virtually certain that a message is duplicated and read widely.

The lesson? Email messages should be composed with care. They should be specifically addressed only to those who need to read them – careless copies to others should be avoided. Posting to a newsgroup should only be made after careful consideration, and preferably never in a hurry, or while in a state of ill temper. Nothing sensitive or confidential should ever be sent electronically. It may possibly be kept private, but, once posted, this is totally beyond the sender's control. Finally, if you intend to act in a way which is outside the normally accepted rules – by, for example, distributing private messages – you should make this clear to your correspondents in advance.

Choice of language

The question of appropriate language – how to express what you want to say – adds to the difficulties which face the poster of email. Electronic text has limited bandwidth – there are no expressions, no tone of voice, no non-verbal cues, no handwriting style – and so on. The combination of the limited bandwidth allowed by electronic text and the casual nature of many messages can all too easily cause the recipient of a message to misunderstand its meaning. This is a particular risk if a message has been composed and sent in a hurry, or perhaps in a fit of annoyance. Electronic text gives little opportunity for feedback – unlike a telephone conversation, there is no cue to the meaning of a message from the tone of voice of a caller, and initial misunderstandings cannot be rapidly corrected.

The concept of familiar paper-based letter writing also contrasts with the immediacy of electronic communication. The time and effort needed to prepare and send paper-based messages tends to reduce the chance of accidental misunderstandings. For example, writing, addressing and mailing a paper letter on the spur of the moment in response to a temporary annoyance is far more difficult than sending email – and hence less likely.

It is therefore important that senders of email messages are always certain that the text actually reflects what they want to say, and that they are content to be associated with its style and manner. Rereading a message or news item before posting it should be automatic; it is frequently surprising what unnoticed mistakes this may reveal. (Running a spell checker, for instance, is particularly recommended.) When feeling annoyed, it is almost always preferable not to reply to a message or posting immediately, but to wait until feelings have calmed down. Quite apart from the immediate response of an addressee to an ill-chosen reply, any unfortunate choice of words may cause considerable problems later. Your message may be circulated, copied, or stored – in any combination.

Even with these precautions, though, there can be unwanted misunderstandings. For this reason, specific ways to express meaning more clearly in electronic messages and postings have evolved. For example, a joke, or frivolous comment is often indicated by being followed by a 'smiley' face, such as ;-) or one of its many variations. Use of a 'smiley' can defuse a critical comment which might otherwise be taken as a serious statement.

Another precaution to take, if making a public posting of information, is to consider adding a 'spoiler' warning – a message that the posting contains information which some readers may prefer not to see. For example, discussion in Star Trek newsgroups was particularly intense after the announcement of a new series – Star Trek Voyager. A typical posting contained new information, but added a 'spoiler', to warn those preferring to remain uninformed that they should skip this posting:

```
From: [deleted]
Newsgroups: rec.arts.startrek.current
Subject: Generation spoiler... the Sulus.
Date: 30 Aug 1994 18:53:24 -0400
Organization: NandO — The News & Observer online
Message-ID: <340d94$avc@merlin.nando.net>
Reply-To: [deleted]
NNTP-Posting-Host: merlin.nando.net


***SPOILERS AHEAD You Have Been Warned***
```

Sometimes it may be felt necessary to devote a specific part of a public posting as a strong criticism. After considering any legal issues, the conventional way to restrict the danger of misunderstandings is to contain this criticism within a marked area of the message, by using a 'Flame' warning. Whole newsgroups are devoted to 'flames', and abusive comments from other groups are frequently redirected there. A typical flame:

```
... service from the industry generally is
pretty good, but as for [deleted]
FLAME ON
This company have give us the worst
service I have ever seen. Their
representative doesn't even know what
they're supposed to be supplying!
Incompetent bunch of [deleted]!!!
OK, we're stuck with them, but anyone stupid
enough to consider buying from [deleted]
should burn the money instead!!!
FLAME OFF
That feels better! Does anyone know where
I could find ...
```

Use of such a warning does not, of course, totally remove the danger of an infuriated response, but it may help to separate public perception of your views on a particular subject from you as a person. However, although the Internet is generally tolerant of individuals who criticize, it would be very unwise to assume adding 'flame on/off' to an abusive posting would be an adequate protection against libel. A report[1] of the award of $40 000 to an academic in a Supreme Court action against defamation in a news posting, quoted a lawyer involved:

> Computer users who use these world-wide bulletin-boards should be aware that they could be exposing themselves to defamation actions. It's an informal system where people say quite personal things, but making allegations of paedophilia and bullying is going too far.

In a later case[2] a writ was issued by one physicist against another, following alleged defamation in an Internet newsgroup. Comments from specialist lawyers made it clear that a 'posted' insult to a colleague is not merely read by a very large potential audience, but by a very specific section of the public: one that is acutely interested in the victim's field. Publication to such a specialist audience could potentially cause 'colossal professional damage', a factor which of course greatly influences the outcome and awards in a libel case.

Publication of personal information can be embarrassing, as well as legally unwise. Consider a submission for the Most Embarrassing Misposting, during a discussion held on the Internet newsgroup `alt.folklore.computers`.

> On the T— internal mail network, a girl sent out a joke to the distribution list `DL.HUMOR` (the equivalent of [the Internet group] `rec.humor`). The joke itself was so-so, but it had an attachment. The T— mail system doesn't copy messages when you answer them, it includes a network-wide pointer to the original message instead. This particular joke had been forwarded to her by her lover (who lived in a different continent), and the attachment was an extremely explicit love letter.
>
> Due to user interface bugs in the T— mail system, it was possible to forward a message like this and not realize that the attachment was still there (paging down brought the message 'There is no further text below').
>
> The first person to notice the misposting was somebody in Australia. He called the girl (in Sunnyvale CA) and asked if she had really intended to send out the message. She re-read the joke, decided that something in it was offensive to people in the West Pacific, and rephrased it without geographical connotations, sending it out with the attachment again.
>
> The consequences of this misposting were catastrophic. Both the girl and her lover got fired, ostensibly for other reasons. The morale at T— dropped to a (then) all-time low. The bug is still in the mail system.

As discussed under legal problems, later in this chapter, the legal position concerning the role of universities and other local operators, who act as forwarders of information and together make up the Internet, is still contentious. Should transmitting information which may be libellous prove to be illegal, it is possible that a court may decide to impose penalties on an information transmitter as well as on the person who generated offending email. For a whole range of reasons, therefore, it clearly pays to consider carefully before making a public or private posting which may be interpreted unfavourably.

Junk email

Because sending electronic mail is so easy, the dangers of receiving mail that you did not ask for, and did not want, increase. Consider a heartfelt posting from one victim:

```
From: [deleted]
Newsgroups: uk.net,uk.misc
Subject: Junk Email - Death of Internet predicted,
blah etc
```

Date: 31 Aug 1994 00:23:21 GMT

All - has anyone noticed a sudden increase in the
traffic of 'junk' email ? This is something I've
normally dismissed as another one of these 'Imminent
Death of the Internet Predicted' scare stories we get
every month or so, until of course it happens to me
twice in so many weeks.

First of all I get an (unsolicited) email from some
individual suggesting the setting up of an
organisation for WWW 'Shop' providers with a huge cc
list. Within days I'm getting a huge number of emails
with replies like 'Yes' or 'Here's my URL', as
everyone hits 'Reply to all Recipients'.

Eventually it gets turned into a mailing list, so I
can unsubscribe and resubscribe from a separate
account. (And as an aside, I'm also starting to get
mails saying 'You've been automatically subscribed to
'Blah-L'.

Annoying if Blah-L is uninteresting, but at least I
can unsubscribe).

Within days, another one starts up with *43* ccs from
a '[deleted]@Finesse.COM' asking for information for a
book. Again, this was of interest to me, but again all
of a sudden I'm receiving tons of unsolicited mail as
all these 43 odd people start sending in their
replies. The sooner this turns into a mailing list the
better. And if it doesn't ? Well, it's time to write
some mail filtering software I guess (or at least turn
on vacation until they get the hint !).

Why am I sharing this with you ? Therapeutic really -
it's starting to get to me. Am I alone in this ? Does
this happen to anyone else ?

```
[deleted]@demon - I notice you've been in the cc list
for both of these - what's your opinion ?

That's better, I've got it out of my system !
```

The lessons are obvious. Accurately identify all recipients of your postings, and try to avoid the mistakes this posting has illustrated – especially the inclusion of enormous numbers of 'ccs' to your mail. Remember, it is more than just unfortunate if email you send is viewed as junk; getting your name added to someone's mail filtering program is very much easier than getting it taken off.

A final point, which is particularly important, is that it is helpful to always read a newsgroup carefully for some time before making a posting there. This is probably the single most important recommendation to anyone intending to post publicly. Studying a group in this way gives a flavour of what is accepted, and what is considered inappropriate there. It also reduces the chances of personal flames – or worse – being directed at you for a misjudged posting. No one can predict what will attract flames. They will always be less likely, however, if your posting shows not only an understanding of a group's aims, but also the usual format of postings there. Not all users of electronic media are kind and considerate to those perceived as inappropriately foolish, and you can be sure that someone, somewhere, will be only too pleased to make this clear to you.

Guidelines

In sending electronic messages and newsgroup postings:[3]

- *Create single-subject messages whenever possible.*
  This makes your meaning clearer, and, if your message is to be forwarded, the process is simplified.
- *Assume that any message you send is permanent.*
  However temporary you may consider your mail ought to be, you cannot dictate this view to your audience, who may keep it indefinitely.
- *Have in mind a model of your intended audience.*
  Make sure that the language you use (for example, the use of slang) is appropriate; always keeping in mind the people who will read

your email helps in writing it.

- *Keep the list of recipients and ccs to a minimum.*
  Do what you can to minimize unwanted email.
- *Separate opinion from non-opinion, and clearly label each.*
  If challenged, you should always be able to adequately defend what you have written. Unjustified speculation can be expensive.
- *If you must express emotion in a message, clearly label it.*
  Remember – Flame on! (and off!)
- *Other content labels are useful.*
  'Spoilers' and 'smilies' help to indicate what you have in mind.
- *Think about the level of formality you put in a message.*
  The importance given to a message by recipients is likely to be in proportion to the attention and care taken to produce it.
- *Identify yourself and your affiliations clearly.*
  A message may come from virtually anywhere or anyone, so readers of your email need to know who you are. The absence of a printed letterhead means your message must contain sufficient data to appropriately 'place' you.
- *Be selective in broadcasts for information.*
  Posting general queries to inappropriate newsgroups uses net bandwidth, annoys users, and, generally, does not work, either. Select a newsgroup carefully to obtain the best response to a query, and do not post unnecessarily – someone else may have just asked the same question.
- Do not insult or criticize third parties without giving them a chance to respond.

Other issues in the use of electronic communication

So far we have considered the everyday use of conventional electronic communication, both through person-to-person email, and by posting an article to the wider readership of a newsgroup. However well the system may operate in normal use, there are unfortunately other, broader, issues which must always be kept in mind. These concern the techniques by which electronic communication may be used illegally, or in ways which undermine the responses users may have anticipated.

Security – email is not secure

Many users automatically treat electronic mail as they would paper mail

– specifically, they believe that once a letter is sealed and posted, its contents will remain confidential. This is not necessarily so. Email is often sent directly from one user to another, and is then, in theory, confidential to them both.

As was described earlier, if the subject of an email message is of wider interest, it is of course easy to send an identical message to a large number of individuals; this may be arranged by sending copies of a letter to each individual, or by maintaining a 'mailing list', where a message posted to a specific list is automatically distributed to each individual whose email address is on the list.

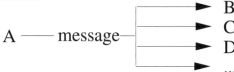

The arrangements may differ, but to sender and recipients, email appears to pass directly from one to the other. What actually happens is normally slightly more complex:

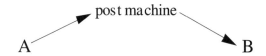

This distinction is important, because, once it is understood that there is always at least one *intermediary* stage between A and B, it can readily be appreciated that a message from A can be intercepted. A message which is apparently from A can even be triggered by someone else, provided that they are able to persuade the post machine to generate a suitable message header. A totally new message may thus be created, a message which looks to a recipient exactly as though it was created by a particular user, even though that user may never have seen it. (An example of such a forged message is given in Appendix B.)

Interception and false generation of mail in this way can be easily done by anyone with the ability to carry out simple commands, and the authorization to do so. It may happen at any point where the message from A is relayed to B through a mail host. (In the case of false messages, it may of course take place, literally, anywhere.)

If access can be gained to the user's home machine – perhaps through a compromised password – an apparently 'genuine' message may be sent. Here is an example of such a posting, made to the normally placid Internet news group rec.antiques.

```
From: sand@netaxs.com (Pritt Sand)
Newsgroups: rec.antiques
Subject: Re: What the hell - antique group?
Date: 25 Jul 1994 18:17:15 GMT
Organization: Net Access - Philadelphia's Internet


John Doe (jdoe@netaxs.com) wrote:
> What the hell, am antique group? Sorry guys, but someone
> had to say it. It just I couldn't believe my eyes when I
> saw this group. Isn't there better things to use precious
> net bandwidth on?
>
> jdoe@netaxs.com


On July 22nd from 03:00 to 04:00 GMT, someone used
compromised passwords from six of our bbs accounts to
post about 25 articles to these groups. As hundreds of
you have pointed out most of these articles were
obscene, inappropriate, and in some cases illegal.
Some contained a "Make Money Fast" scam article with
our mailing address, while one advertised free phone
sex from our customer service line.


The owners of these compromised accounts were not
involved in the postings in any way, and are not at
any fault in the matter.


We regret the incident, and are taking additional
measures to improve password security to help prevent
future such problems.
```

```
Please direct followup comments to our postmaster, and
spare the unfortunate owners of the compromised
accounts, and the other readers of these newsgroups.

    Sincerely,
            - the NETAXS Customer Support Team,
            - and Pritt Sand (system administration)
(postmaster@netaxs.com)
```

I mentioned earlier in this chapter a request in `soc.culture.scientists` for comments on maintaining the confidentiality of private email messages. One response to this request was particularly thought provoking:

> There are other issues, however (as at least one author noted), regarding the inherent public nature of email. For instance, any system administrator on any of the nodes through which email passes could easily look at it, sift through it selectively, copy it, and so on. This is why email has limited use for things like company-confidential materials, if it is known that the email passes through public channels.
>
> Furthermore, there are no guarantees against 'inside' snooping; for example, by one's own management, by a competing researcher in your lab, or whatever.

Although the chances of any individual message being forged, or even altered, are probably very small, the risk is nevertheless a real one, and should always be kept in mind. The lesson is important. No email message should be assumed to be authentic unless it has been checked. Such checking is clearly especially relevant when the contents of the message are of a contentious nature, where comments appear to be out of character, or where a message makes unexpected demands or statements.

Plainly, actually forging such mail is hard to defend ethically.

Legal problems

As we have discussed earlier, those responsible for supporting and maintaining user services are naturally concerned with issues such as user file confidentiality, and general data protection. These may lead to particular difficulties.

Potential conflict with authority

Security measures in force on most sites deal with preservation of data from unwanted intrusion, and show awareness of the need to maintain the confidence of users in the security of their system, files and data. However, there are increasing risks of conflict between system administrators and official agencies. Demands may be made for access to user files without proper justification, or even without legal authority. Demands of this sort may come at system administrators from any direction – from their own management, from a politician, or even from the police.

One case which clearly illustrated the problems was the reaction of authorities at the University of Western Ontario to police demands for access to files in a user's account. (Appendix C gives a full picture of this very interesting case.) In summary – the university immediately did everything it was asked. Its Computer Security Officer was actually quoted as saying he was not interested in even discussing whether a file was legal or not – if the police said it was illegal, that was good enough for him.

The important point is, as usual, not whether the Western Ontario system administrators were right or wrong to respond as they did. What is important is that they may have responded automatically, and without apparent reference to any agreed ethical codes or standards.

The attitude of administrators to their safeguarding of other people's data is central to their job. If a lack of previous planning or consideration makes abdicating responsibility in this way inevitable, what are the wider implication for users? The unfortunate administrators at Western Ontario University are certainly not alone. As Karen Adams, executive director of the Canadian Library Association, put it, when commenting on this case:[4]

> The promise of the information superhighway is that we all become librarians and reporters. The danger right now is most people don't understand the responsibilities that come with their new roles.

An automatic assumption that the police must always be right is a dangerous one for civil liberties. A professional librarian may, as Karen Adams felt, have been less likely than the Ontario system administrators to turn over personal information to the police; but librarians have a tradition of protecting individual academic freedoms. Traditions, of course, take time to develop. We have no similar tradition within computing, and will have to wait for one. There is nothing, though, to prevent system administrators and others developing appropriate individual ethical views, together with an agreed official policy. When the police call, it may be too late to develop anything.

Publishing

As was briefly mentioned earlier, there is, currently, no clear ruling on whether an information supplier is liable when forwarding an electronic posting which is subsequently found to be libellous. There is, of course, no such organization as 'Internet'; this is the name given to an association of autonomous linked computer networks. 'Posted' information is passed through the Internet by moving from one network to another, at each stage being both stored and forwarded.

The arrangements have worked well for years, due perhaps to the high proportion of computer specialists who were involved in use of the Internet. However, large numbers of inexperienced users from a wide variety of backgrounds are now obtaining and using access to the Internet. Their approach to postings may be less predictable, but their messages must be distributed in the same manner, by moving from one network to another. What is the status of an information supplier when the information it passes on proves to be libellous or otherwise illegal?

A company which distributes paper documents in this way is viewed as a publisher, and there have been several attempts to consider distributors of electronic information as 'publishers'. A 1993 American case – *Cubby v. CompuServe* – illustrates the problem well.

In this case, CompuServe (which is a computer network, charging fees to subscribers) was named as second Defendant where an allegedly defamatory article was published in one of its many newsgroups.

CompuServe successfully argued that it could not be held to have 'published' (in the normal sense) the defaming statement. It maintained that because it operated such a large number of newsgroups, it would be impossible to read through each article in each group before publicly 'posting' it.

A similar argument on policy consideration grounds may prove to be a successful defence under English law. However, there are other considerations, and it would probably depend on the particular circumstances of the information provider – i.e. how many newsgroups it carried; and, possibly, even whether the article was sent to the information provider from a remote site, or whether the author resided at the particular site in question.

Several Internet-connected sites in the UK refuse to distribute certain specialist newsgroups, usually those connected to sexual behaviour; but of course any newsgroup may at any time carry a posting considered offensive by someone.

Conclusions

This chapter has looked at the distribution of information electronically, through email and posting to newsgroups. It has examined the potential problems involved in such postings, and has made a number of recommendations, summarized under the Guidelines heading. Finally, the question of illegal and unauthorized use was examined.

Only after its pitfalls are recognized and taken into account should electronic mail be used. It is not private, and can be corrupted or even forged. Despite its fragile appearance, it is not ephemeral, either; long after an originator may have forgotten its existence, copies of mail can be widely distributed and stored.

Personal issues, such as writing style, and even emotion, may affect the appearance of email, and consequently the way in which it might be received and viewed. Wider implications, including the questionable legal status of electronic information, also need consideration.

Electronic mail has very considerable advantages, but its limitations need to be thoroughly understood.

Questions

1. How is sending an electronic message different from sending an ordinary letter or memo?
2. Consider ways in which your ethical views may affect your use of email. Would there be any differences in your approach to posting to newsgroups and posting personal mail?
3. If you were able to forge email, what would stop you doing so?
4. If you use email, how long do you normally take to reply to a message? What reasons might there be to delay a reply?

Notes

[1] In the *West Australian*, Saturday 2 April 1994.
[2] Reported in the *Times Higher*, 26 August 1994.
[3] This list is adapted, with kind permission of the Rand Corporation, from the paper 'Toward an ethics and etiquette for electronic mail', Rand Corporation paper R-3283-NSF/RC, 1985. Despite its date, the paper is still well worth reading in full.
[4] *eye* magazine, Toronto, Canada, 19 May 1994. The article is quoted at length in Appendix C.

10

Summary

This final chapter brings together the main issues that have been raised in the book, and makes some specific and general suggestions for ethical working in the area of computer science.

The beginning

Moral philosophy, or ethics, as it is more generally known, is undeniably perceived by many as an 'arts' rather than a 'science' subject. It is consequently understandable that computer scientists may be dubious about the potential advantages of spending time in studying it. After all, there is little enough time to study the essential core aspects of our field, without wasting time on something which is not only peripheral to the work, but may not even be proper science. Chapter 1 considered the subject of ethics in general terms, before tackling the question of why computer scientists need to spend time thinking about ethical issues.

It concluded that there were legal and practical reasons why a knowledge of ethics was appropriate. Incentives included the necessity for practitioners to comply with computer-related legislation, and, of course, to respond appropriately to public pressure. Both clients and employers appeared to prefer a professional computer scientist known to act ethically.

However, the most important conclusion was that a person should not unthinkingly accept standards from outside. Individuals should instead develop their own views of what is, and is not, ethical. Once this had been accomplished, operating within consistent ethical standards will not only help in professional practice, but will provide potentially significant personal incentives, as well.

Following through

The next chapter took up the question of developing a personal ethical code, and carried it further. It began by examining where personal views might come from, and on what they are likely to be based. Influences on individuals are not always obvious, and may come from unexpected directions. What may seem at first to be a genuine 'personal' view or opinion, might in fact turn out, instead, to be the reflection of something quite different.

In practice, working definitions of ethical conduct may sometimes merely reflect the current needs of an employer. Unless you can be conscious of where beliefs come from, therefore, you may not appreciate that they have been influenced from outside. However understandable such unawareness may be, passing responsibility to an employer is clearly not a responsible way to build individual ethical standards.

A number of mechanisms by which someone might be influenced were examined. These ranged from the attitudes of close family and friends to the wider pressures of society. Figure 2.1 brought together the various levels of potential pressure which might influence the behaviour of an individual, and illustrated some potential pressures for individuals to accept certain views as appropriate.

Working out what might be an 'ethical' problem in computing may be far from straightforward. Chapter 3 tackled this issue. It began by considering a traditional approach to ethics, suggesting that these would be better replaced by a more focused use of examples. It then looked at general ways in which ethical problems might be identified, and gave pointers to help in identifying ethical problems. It also suggested ways of ruling out problems which could not be usefully categorized as 'ethical'.

We then looked in more detail at the identification of ethical issues, and, in particular, the criteria for individual definition. We stressed the need to use structured analysis in applying such criteria, and described some ways in which such analysis could be applied. One proposed suggestion was to develop a form of cognitive 'filter', to help bring those issues that were important to an individual to their conscious attention.

The chapter concluded with investigation of some typical 'ethical' problems in the field of computing, and discussion of what they might involve.

Applying an ethical code

Once a problem has been appropriately identified, the next stage in the process of resolution is obviously to decide what should be done. Chapter 4 examined ways in which an appropriate resolution of the problem might be achieved. A process of considered analysis was deemed an essential response to all potential ethical problems; analysis should assist in accurately identifying possible choices, and help predict the likely results of following them. On the other hand, refusing to consider an ethical problem can, in reality, be a different, and far less satisfactory, way of taking action about it.

The chapter included examples of 'ethical' problems and decisions, and looked at both the immediate relevance of problem resolution and the potential longer term effects. There was a practical discussion on how people reach decisions, including external and internal pressures to respond. Help in reaching a decision can be sought from various directions – including professional organizations and colleagues, as well as the important area of personal support. When the outcome of an ethical problem might affect them, there is particular importance in involving partner and family in the decision process.

Finally, the pressures which might encourage (or prevent) specific actions were discussed – the attitudes of friends and family were probably the most important here. Finally, the whole process of ethical decision making was brought together as a flow chart.

Computing potentially covers many fields. The range of ethical problems which might be encountered by a practitioner in computing is consequently enormous. Chapter 5 examined a variety of different situations where working with computers could throw up obvious, and not so obvious, ethical problems, and looked at them in detail.

Although the cases considered were very different in scale and location, several generally applicable pointers nevertheless emerged from this discussion:

- Clarify the situation before deciding anything.
- Be aware of your responsibilities to employer and client – and yourself.
- Respect the views of others.
- Be prepared to consider an alternative point of view.
- Wider, non-technical issues may be relevant to your work.
- Ethical responsibility cannot be transferred.

Legal and professional issues

All computing use is constrained in some way by statute. Chapter 6 looked at the development of computer-related regulatory law within the UK, before focusing specifically on the 1984 Data Protection Act and the 1990 Computer Misuse Act. Everyone working with computers needs to have at least a working knowledge of this legislation, and summaries of both Acts were presented to aid comprehension. The chapter ended with a synopsis of other legislation relevant to computer users.

While the behaviour of those working with computers is bound by statute law, general computing practice is additionally both supported and controlled by the codes of conduct issued by concerned professional organizations. Chapter 7 looked at the reasons why formal professional codes of conduct exist, and discussed how, as well as being of particular service to members of the relevant society or association, their existence could be of considerable benefit to the wider computing profession.

At present the only UK code of conduct is that of the BCS. Knowledge of this code was felt to be crucial to any UK practitioners in software engineering, whether or not they were members of the BCS. Using the BCS code as a specific example, the chapter examined in detail how each section of an ethical code could be related to actual practice. It also looked briefly at common expectations of employers concerning professional standards.

Chapter 8 looked closely at the ethical problems and responsibilities involved in maintaining an efficient computer system. Within any organization, there should be a general understanding of its use of computer systems. In particular, there is a need for staff working with computer systems to be adequately informed about a company's position on computer-related issues – such as mail monitoring.

It was also argued that there was a need for employees to take responsibility for their views. The sometimes thorny relationship between systems administrators and managers was discussed, with the conclusion that, whatever the particular philosophy of the organization, there should be informed awareness on the part of employer, systems administrator and system users of local rules and expectations.

Some potential ethical issues involving bulletin boards were then considered, and parallels drawn between a systems administrator and the 'sysop' of a BBS. There is a need for both professional and amateur systems operators to acknowledge ethical issues, and to be attentive to the growing political pressures to act in ways seen as 'responsible'.

Chapter 8 concluded with a discussion on 'hacking' and the frequently associated issues of computer viruses and software theft.

Chapter 9 examined the way in which personally generated data is distributed, and identified points of potential ethical conflict in the generation and transmission of both personal electronic mail (email) and the wider distributions of Internet news groups.

Personally generated information does not just pass through bulletin boards; distribution of such data plays a major role in virtually all computer systems. Sometimes the information is communicated directly between individuals, or within a business; sometimes it is intended for a wider audience. After discussion of the issues, some suggested guidelines for the use of electronic mail were proposed. Despite the ease with which mail may be generated, discretion and judgement are undoubtedly needed for electronic communication.

The chapter concluded with a brief examination of some legal risks. Some risks were to users, partly through pressure on systems administrators, but the growing potential risk to electronic forwarders of information, who are potentially 'publishing' institutions, was also stressed.

Conclusions

In this book I have drawn on information from a very wide area, and have considered the subject of ethics from a variety of different perspectives. Although earlier experiences had helped convince me of the importance of holding an individual ethical code, as a computer scientist I was initially sceptical about the relevance of ethics to CS. Happily, the more closely I looked at the subject the clearer the position became, and the more computer scientists I found who believed ethical issues were important to their work.

This was particularly interesting, because, when I first decided to write this book, I 'advertised' on the Internet for views and experiences relating to ethical issues in computer science. Instead of the anticipated handful of replies, I was overwhelmed with responses, most clearly displaying evidence that considerable time had been spent on them. Most, but by no means all, were in favour of the introduction of ethics to computer science; a typical negative view raised as many questions as it answered:

> As a database administrator, as long as I ignore the 'content' of the database I have no ethical problems.

One newsgroup alone – `comp.databases.theory` – generated so many replies that I collected them together, and innocently posted a message offering the file to those who were interested. In the first two days 147 requests arrived, together with many further personal experiences and opinions. Several responses were of course included in Chapter 5, but one reply – by no means the longest – is worth quoting at greater length. It is from a specialist in database design, and covers many of the issues which have been discussed here.

It is my feeling that a major ethics question is: how does one balance the need for immediate solutions to problems versus the need to take a thorough, life cycle approach to the solution of the problem?

Most of us have been in situations (all of mine are this way) in which the problem to be solved via a database and application program was apparent, critical, and long overdue. It is *very* easy to promise the world to the customer tomorrow, skip some of the up front analysis and run right into system development. You end up designing the database by virtue of what you want the *application* to look like. Sometimes this works, but most of the time it does not. Major problems are often encountered later in the life cycle when system upgrading or system integration is required. The new system capabilities won't fit or another system can't be integrated because the database wasn't designed correctly.

On the other hand, timely responses to customer requirements are a real issue. The lifetime of systems in this rapidly advancing technological world yields many systems obsolete before they are even finished! (Whom among us can't think of numerous examples of this!)

So, wherein lies the compromise? I would venture to guess that this is one of those where you can't simply say the answer is x. I think that what we must instil in students that the responsibility for balancing proper design with responsiveness is in their hands. *but*, I also believe that a student must be taught minimum standards for proper design techniques.

This means that if an analyst is using, say, relational databases, he/she *must* be knowledgeable of relational theory, comfortable with the concept of normalization, and willing to allow this knowledge to flow through their work. In other words, theory and concepts become less rules we apply and more tools that we work with. As a carpenter doesn't say, 'Aha, here is my hammer, I think I shall pound some nails' but rather 'I need to pound some nails and my hammer is the correct tool.', a programmer must say, 'I am developing a relational database and normalization is the right tool'.

If this approach is used then proper design flows out of the process rather than taking effort to implement. It changes the way we think rather than hovering over us waiting to cause distress later.

This view is both personal, and thoroughly professional. It clearly comes from knowledge, experience and the application of individual standards, and brings together many of the themes of this book.

Consider your views and opinions; how they were reached, and how much they actually reflect what *you* believe, not what it may be convenient for others to encourage you to believe. Be aware of the need to consider your work in relation to wider issues, and, when confronted with an issue which might be defined in your terms as ethical, always think it through. Consider alternatives, consult those who can offer support or appropriate advice, and, finally, reach a decision which you are able to justify – and with which you can be comfortable.

I hope this book has encouraged you to consider studying 'ethics': an arts subject which has professional relevance to the work of a computer scientist. It may have wider benefits, too.

Questions

1. Chapter 1's questions asked you to write down three or four words which you felt appropriately described the subject of 'ethics'. Do this again; and compare these new notes with your earlier views.

Appendix A

Data Protection Act, 1984

It is important that subjects of personal information held on computer systems appreciate what information is held about them, and for what purposes it is stored. As described in Chapter 6, there is a legal and ethical responsibility for a data holder to make subjects aware of these issues.

The Open University provides an excellent example of good practice. This appendix reproduces (with permission) the informative text given to all new Open University students, telling them about the storage of information concerning them and explaining the purposes to which it may be put.

'Personal Data' Information – Open University

Any information provided by you may be held by the University on computer in accordance with the Data Protection Act 1984. The ways in which the University may use this information are contained in the enclosed literature.

You have the right of access to your personal records held on computer and enquiries should be addressed to . . .

[After this legal statement, the accompanying literature contains fuller details:]

Use of personal information

The Data Protection Act places responsibilities upon users of personal information held on computer. The Act sets out certain principles on how information is obtained, stored and disclosed. The first of these principles states that information must be obtained fairly.

The Data Protection Registrar feels that information is only obtained fairly if the person giving it is told about any way in which it may be used which he or she may not expect. This is to enable people to decide whether or not they want to give the information.

What does the University use personal information for?

When you apply for a course we store information about you in our computer records. Details of the purposes for which we hold information and the bodies to which we may disclose it are listed in the Register of Data Users and Computer Bureaux. This is a public register kept by the Data Protection Registrar and you may inspect it free of charge. If you wish to apply for subject access (that is, for a copy of any data which the University holds about you on computer) you should apply in writing to the Data Protection Co-ordinator. A fee of £8.00 is payable for each subject access request.

The main use of the information that we hold will be obvious e.g. the processing of applications and the provision of student support services. However, we may use information in the following ways which may not be obvious to you.

Research and statistical analysis

We may use your information to ask for your help in O.U. market and research surveys in order to help with planning and to improve the University's teaching services and systems. We also provide information about students (but not names) to other bodies e.g. government departments for statistical analysis; and the University itself produces statistics which are published.

Marketing

Your information may be used to tell you about goods or services you may find useful. This might be details of other study opportunities or of goods or services offered by companies to O.U. students e.g. the Visa card offered by —— Bank plc or goods marketed by the O.U. Students' Association.

Fundraising

We may use your information to tell you about the University's fundraising needs and activities and invite you to contribute to O.U. initiatives and projects.

Disclosures

Personal data will only be disclosed in accordance with the terms of the University's registrations under the Data Protection Act. For example, the University is required by the Higher Education Funding Council to provide information on students (including names) to the Higher Education Statistical Agency (HESA). HESA is managed by the Universities and Colleges of Higher Education of the UK and operates under strict rules of disclosure which are registered with the Data Protection Registrar. Under these rules HESA will not provide the names of students to Government departments or other third parties.

Note

Information in this Appendix is reproduced by kind permission of the Open University.

Appendix B

Anatomy of a forgery

Not all news postings are authentic. This appendix contains an example of a posting which looked OK, but was not.

Netcom is an organization offering, among much else, Internet connection to modem users. A Netcom user, acting as a beta tester, appeared to have misused the system. A forger, pretending to be Netcom official 'Ralph Evans', deliberately fanned the flames.

To understand the text, it is necessary to know that Internet newsgroup posting conventions normally mark material from an earlier posting which is included in a later one. Such marking is usually done by beginning each quoted line with a '>' sign. Each further level of quotation is marked by an additional '>'.

A line beginning:

```
>> quoted material
```

therefore shows a nested quotation – in effect, a quoted quote.

Note the headers on each message; the first is *forged*, the second genuine.

All spelling, grammar and punctuation errors from the original text have been retained for reasons of authenticity.

A forged posting

```
Newsgroups: alt.sources.mac
Path:
ukc!uknet!bhamcs!bham!warwick!slxsys!pipex!howland.reston.an
s.net!spool.mu.edu!news.cs.indiana.edu!catalyst@netcom.com
From: catalyst-remailer@netcom.com
```

Subject: Netcom "censorship": MOSTLY LIES
Message-ID: <199407201851. LAA25879@mail. netcom. com>
Sender: root@news.cs.indiana.edu (Operator)
Followups-To: news.admin.policy
Reply-To: <support@netcom.com>
Organization: Computer Science, Indiana University
Comment: This message is NOT from the address on the'From:
'line; it is from an anonymous remailing service. Please
report problem mail to catalyst@netcom.com.
Date: Wed, 20 Jul 1994 11:51:57 -0700
Remailed-By: Remailer <catalyst-remailer@netcom.com>
Lines: 53

In article <andrysCsx25L.9Jz@netcom.com>,
Andrys D Basten <andrys@netcom.com> wrote:
>In article <evnsCstqDF.7Ar@netcom.com>,
>Ralph Evans <ralph@evans.com> wrote:
>
>>Being accepted into a beta test program puts one in a
>>relationship of trust and confidence with the vendor. To
>>slam a beta publicly is beyond the pale.
>>It's that simple.
>
>Not that simple at all.
>The upshot, normally, would be that the opinion-giver (the
>2nd-wave beta-testing was described as 'non-confidential')
>might not be invited into future beta-testing. Closing an
>account is altogether too extreme and an action not
>appropriate to public criticism of a beta for which there
>was no NDA. I usually sign NDA's for beta's but there was
>none that I received for this one. I gave my pro's and
>con's here, on this board, as well.
>
>I'm pretty shocked.
>

Probably because you were sucked in by the propaganda
distortions here. She was not censored. Here account was
closed with a banner message to call Netcom. That's common
for a variety of reasons (someone send in a complain about

your postings, or whatever). When she called and showed that she was submissive and apologetic about her comments, her account was restored, after it was established that she would refrain from saying anything negative about Netcom in the future.

Whether closing an account in order to show a user their "proper place" and see how much they grovel over the phone after discovering in shock they have no access to their personal files and email, in my view, a judgement call, not the slaughter of small dogs and children in the public square. If some of the responses (not yours) in messages here weren't so ludicrous they'd be pathetic. Stephanie is a lot like MOST rape victims: was probably asking for it. (Notice I am only saying MOST rape victims, not ALL, so don't send me idiotic flames about my supposed "insensitivity".)

This whole thing reminds me of the old aphorism that academic politics is the most vicious kind because so little is involved.

Ralph
evns@netcom.com
—

The values that define our common-sense world are under assault. Some have taken to extremes the spurious notion of freedom without responsibility, and are trying to tear down moral guardrails. Those who live on the shoulders are told by their pals that they are in the middle of the road. Nothing is wrong any more (except, of course, conservative thoughts and expressions).

The (authentic) response:

Newsgroups: alt.sources.mac
Path: ukc!uknet!lyra. csx.cam. ac.uk!warwick! slxsys!pipex!
howland.reston.ans.net!math.ohio-state.edu!magnus.acs.ohio-
state.edu!csn!csus.edu!netcom.com!evns
From: evns@netcom.com (Ralph Evans)

Subject: Re: Netcom "censorship": MOSTLY LIES
Message-ID: <evnsCtAyn4.Moz@netcom.com>
Reply-To: ralph@evans.com (Ralph Evans)
Organization: DSI/USCRPAC
References: <199407201851. LAA25879@mail. netcom. com>
<evnsCtAwuw. HCL@netcom.com>
Date: Thu, 21 Jul 1994 18:13:51 GMT
Lines: 108

Here is a dissection of the forgery. What the forger did
was to stitch together outrageous statements I never made
with some material from netcom.general. Note that the
presenting issue for the discussion was a beta tester who
posted pans of the beta publicly. I took the position that
this was unethical; others took the position that it was
not. She then had her account put on hold with a message to
call her net provider after the provider was unsuccesful at
reaching her by phone. The provider thought her posts might
be a deliberate plot by the competition to blacken their
name.
When she called they established that this was not the case,
restored her account, and gave her a free month of service
as a kind of apology. I took the position that this was a
judgement call within the user agreement of the provider,
others took the position that this was an outrage of the
worst kind. The issue was the subject of extensive
discussion in the service's private newsgroup. It has been
beaten to death and I give the background only to permit
readers to figure out what's going on.

From support@netcom.com Thu Jul 21 10:35:37 PDT 1994

The above line is forged

In article <andrysCsx25L.9Jz@netcom.com>,
Andrys D Basten <andrys@netcom.com> wrote:
>In article <evnsCstqDF.7Ar@netcom.com>,
>Ralph Evans <ralph@evans.com> wrote:
>

>>Being accepted into a beta test program puts one in a
>>relationship of trust and confidence with the vendor. To
>>slam a beta publicly is beyond the pale.
>>It's that simple.
>
>Not that simple at all.
>The upshot, normally, would be that the opinion-giver
>(the 2nd-wave beta-testing was described as 'non-
>confidential') might not be invited into future beta-
>testing. Closing an account is altogether too extreme and
>an action not appropriate to public criticism of a beta for
>which there was no NDA. I usually sign NDA's for beta's
>but there was none that I received for this one. I gave my
>pro's and con's here, on this board, as well.

The above material is authentic

>I'm pretty shocked.

Probably because you were sucked in by the propaganda
distortions here. She was not censored. Here account was
closed with a banner message to call Netcom. That's common
for a variety of reasons

The above material is authentic

(someone send in a complain about your postings, or
whatever). When she called and showed that she was
submissive and apologetic about her comments, her account
was restored, after it was established that she would
refrain from saying anything negative about Netcom in the
future.

The above material is FORGED

Whether closing an account in order to show a user their
"proper place" and see how much they grovel over the phone
after discovering in shock they have no access to their
personal files and email, in my

The above material is FORGED

view, a judgement call, not the slaughter of small dogs and
children in the public square. If some of the responses (not
yours) in messages here weren't so ludicrous they'd be
pathetic.

The above material is genuine, but taken from an entirely
different paragraph saying that putting her account on hold
was, in my view, a judgement call.

Stephanie is a lot like MOST rape victims: was probably
asking for it. (Notice I am only saying MOST rape victims,
not ALL, so don't send me idiotic flames about my supposed
"insensitivity".)

The above material is FORGED

This whole thing reminds me of the old aphorism that
academic politics is the most vicious kind because so little
is involved.

Ralph
evns@netcom.com
—

The values that define our common-sense world are under
assault. Some have taken to extremes the spurious notion of
freedom without responsibility, and are trying to tear down
moral guardrails. Those who live on the shoulders are told
by their pals that they are in the middle of the road.
Nothing is wrong any more (except, of course, conservative
thoughts and expressions).

The above material is genuine, and taken from other
innocuous material.
—

Ralph Evans' comments are changed to *italic* for emphasis. (His original posting just marked them.)

Thanks to 'Ralph Evans', of Netcom, for permission to reproduce
this correspondence.

Appendix C

Internet and the police

A Canadian legal case, the Karla Homolka trial, created considerable interest and discussion on the net and elsewhere. Although the local Canadian Press was restricted by court order in what it could print, Canadians with Internet access were able to learn from other reports – principally in the US – what was happening on their own doorsteps. What happened next is described in this report, dated 19 May 1994, from the *eye* newspaper of Toronto, a paper similar to New York's *Village Voice*.

POLICING THE NEW MEDIA

INTERNET USERS HAVE THEIR LIBERTY THREATENED AS LAW ENFORCEMENT AGENCIES BLUNDER ABOUT TRYING (AND FAILING) TO ENFORCE THE HOMOLKA PRESS BAN

by
K.K. CAMPBELL

Karla Homolka was sentenced to 12 years for manslaughter in the deaths of two teenage girls. The ban on publishing details of her trial was imposed to insure husband Paul Teale a fair trial. But Teale's lawyer opposes the ban.

Homolka's trial has stopped being the story – the story has become the ban itself. There's been nothing new to report about the trial for months, but the story keeps coming back because *the ban* keeps making headlines. Every time the ban causes a magazine to be dramatically pulled from store shelves, every time the ban causes cops to barge into a student's life with unfounded allegations, every time a university censors or snoops out private information, the Homolka case is dragged back into the headlines.

Once there, details are rehashed and new ban-breaking potential results. It's a vicious circle from which the attorney-general's office is desperately trying to extricate itself. It's no coincidence Teale's trial was suddenly moved forward.

Indeed, the attorney-general seems ready to let police operate with a free hand against Ontarians – as one university student found out the hard way.

'ABDUL' SCREWS UP

It began with one of the all-time great gaffes in Internet history. Late last Jan. 31, 21-year-old Toronto student "Abdul" (not his real name) arrived home to his basement apartment from night classes. After a quick bite, he checked his Internet account for e-mail.

To his delight, he found a copy of the revised Karla Homolka computer file in his mailbox – hot-off-the-CPU from a London, Ont., university student. The file was due to be released the next day to the infamous Internet newsgroup alt.fan.karla-homolka. Abdul, the uncrowned prince of the Homolka-Internet underground, got an advance copy.

The file contains a whack of rumors and grisly details about Homolka's secrecy-shrouded quickie-trial last July. Internet convention calls the computer file an "FAQ" – a collection of answers to "Frequently Asked Questions" about a topic. This topic just happens to be the oh-so-controversial Homolka murder trial and the ban surrounding it.

The Homolka FAQ is found wherever computers and Canadians interact. It has undoubtedly been read by tens of thousands of citizens to date.

But none of those readers know the identities of the authors, underground computer activists – only their mysterious aliases: "Abdul, the Electronic Gordon Domm" (abdul@io.com), "Lt Starbuck" (an54835@anon.penet.fi), and "Neal the Trial Ban-Breaker" (an52708@anon.penet.fi).

By 2 a.m., after four hours online, Abdul is ready for sleep. But not before he sends the new FAQ to Toronto's major news outlets – three daily papers and three TV stations. He has e-mail addresses for each.

"I was trying to send the FAQ through an e-mail system in Finland that lets the sender remain completely anonymous," Abdul now recalls. "But it kept bouncing back to me unreceived." Eyes red, Abdul finally decided to send the FAQ through a local fax service. "I sent it, and went to bed. I didn't think anything of it."

Major mistake: Abdul, perhaps overtired, instructed the fax service to send a copy to the six media outlets – as well as a copy to Premier Bob Rae and another to Attorney-General Marion Boyd.

Fatal mistake: Abdul left the real names of Lt Starbuck and himself on the document.

Next morn, sleepy-eyed civil servants found the hefty document awaiting them. The attorney-general's office refuses to comment on its reaction, but suffice to say the shit began shunting through government plumbing – only to emerge three weeks later directly on the head of Lt Starbuck at London's University of Western Ontario.

BATTLE STARBUCK

On Feb. 22, Starbuck, 25, came home from school to find a message waiting: Western's computer and network security officer Reg Quinton wanted him to call. Starbuck did. He was told his Internet account was frozen. He was to meet with London police the next day.

Police?! Mind racing, Starbuck hurried to his home computer. He not only deleted anything remotely related to Homolka from his hard drive but "shredded" it via Norton computer utilities. It was an operation to make any politician proud.

(Though Starbuck is known to the university and OPP, he requests *eye* not use his real name, but rather his alias "Lt Starbuck" – his favorite character from the TV show Battlestar Galactica.)

It seems the attorney-general had notified the OPP, who had passed a copy of the FAQ with Starbuck's real name on it to Detective Sergeant Sandy Wright of the London police. Wright approached Quinton.

"I asked what the police wanted done," Quinton (reggers@julian.uwo.ca) told *eye*. "They wanted the student's account shut down and to meet with him in person. Fine." Quinton called in colleague Dave Martin, who administrates Starbuck's account. No warrant, no subpoena, no problem.

The next afternoon, Starbuck death-marched himself over to Quinton's office in the Natural Science Center. Quinton, Martin and Wright awaited with grim faces.

"During the two-hour interrogation, the police showed me the document Abdul sent the attorney-general," Starbuck recalls. "I stared at it in disbelief, whispering to myself, 'Oh shit.'"

It was game over.

Worse still, the police seemed to think Starbuck himself had sent it because of the way e-mail readers save mail. Not understanding what they were looking at, authorities figured Starbuck had faxed it to them, with his real name, in some moment of stratospheric chutzpah.

Cornered and terrified, Starbuck vowed to tell everything – including the real name of Abdul. Wright asked Starbuck to open his Internet account. He complied – nothing "incriminating" there anyway, his strict policy was to keep no Homolka files in school accounts. Wright said he'd have to inspect Starbuck's home computer. Starbuck explained everything was gone, shredded, but Wright insisted he had to see for himself. (Inexplicably, he set that appointment for the next day – he found nothing.)

WHY ME?

Wright informed Starbuck criminal charges still hung over his head. But as long as he stayed clear of Homolka-mongering and remained cooperative, charges would probably not be laid.

On Feb. 28, Starbuck had his university account restored. For the next three weeks, he forwarded incoming private e-mail from Abdul to Quinton – including a list of about 50 people who received updates of the FAQ. There were five more Western Internet addresses.

One was Wayne Smith (wlsmith@valve.heart.rri.uwo.ca). Smith would publicly complain on Usenet about the whole Western-LPD investigation: "What they are calling cooperation here is intimidation." It's like the old police state mentality: if you have nothing to hide, why won't you take this lie detector test when we ask?

Starbuck says intimidation was a factor. "I cooperated with Quinton for weeks after the event for the sole reason that I was very afraid I'd get charged if I didn't."

Back in Toronto, Abdul was blissfully ignorant of the events in motion in London. He noticed Starbuck didn't seem to answer his e-mail any more. Ironically, it was Wayne Smith's public post just quoted above that alerted him to the monumental gaffe he'd made. He quickly prepared for the police. After all, he was far, far more active than Starbuck had ever been on his best day.

But the knock never came on Abdul's door.

Which still bewilders Starbuck. "There's no rhyme nor reason to it at all. If they're cracking down, why aren't they cracking down anywhere else? Why me? I just edited a computer file. I got sucked into this whole stupid affair and really feel bruised and battered by it."

Abdul believes Starbuck was targeted because Western computer administrators were spineless: "When the police knocked on Quinton's door, it's clear Quinton said, 'Come on in, guys!' "

Another source close to the case put it this way: "The LPD asked Starbuck to bend over – and Quinton applied the vaseline."

The police would definitely need a warrant to peek at Abdul's home computer. And then the issue would erupt into the headlines again.

CHARGED WITH POSSESSION

On March 28, Quinton wrote an "open letter" to the Internet community – which he says was on the "recommendation of the local police." This letter, apparently carrying police sanction, claims mere possession of the FAQ is a crime.

"My understanding is the LPD (and OPP and others) are of the opinion that... to be in possession of such material is to be in violation of the publication ban," Quinton wrote. And such a breach could result in police getting a warrant and seizing entire computer systems.

When *eye* called the LPD's Wright, he repeated this official line, though without the same righteous passion Quinton seems imbued with. Wright said the OPP told him possession of the file constituted a breach of the ban. But OPP Detective Inspector Frank Ryder told *eye* he doesn't know for certain. He only passes information about possible breaches of the trial ban along to local police departments. "It's their investigation, there is no central OPP investigation," Ryder said.

So *eye* called the attorney-general. Spokeswoman Barbara Krever said she couldn't comment on whether possession of the FAQ was a breach of the ban.

In fact, the attorney-general has consistently refused to help Ontarians understand exactly where the Internet fits within the ban. People are left to operate in uncharted territory and law enforcement authorities blunder about, unsure themselves. Meanwhile university students have academic careers, if not their very liberty, threatened.

Criminal lawyer Eddie Greenspan has gone on record saying he does not believe the Internet's Homolka-infotrade breaches the ban. He said accessing Internet files defeats the purpose of the ban but doesn't break the ban. "I don't see anything criminally wrong here," he told *eye*.

Greenspan notes the confusion stems from people thinking the ban applies to details of the trial. The ban concerns publishing that information. Simply cruising out on the Internet and grabbing a copy of the Homolka FAQ is not a breach of the ban; nor is holding it in a university computer account.

"If it comes between Greenspan and Boyd, Ontario's first non-lawyer attorney-general, I'll take Eddie's opinion every time," Abdul says.

Abdul believes courts in the future are going to have to specifically mention the Internet – "or, if they clue in, they will realize bans are obsolete, it's time to change the system to reflect technology." But how many judges have ever confronted a login? Do they understand the raw power of it? Do they understand how it circumvents all censorious power structures?

Former Supreme Court judge Willard Estey said something similar in an April 21 speech: bans in high-profile cases should cease because they just don't work any more. Estey blamed the proximity of the U.S. news media. The Internet compounds the problem exponentially. He said jurors must be trusted to do their jobs – that is, be exposed to various information and not let it affect their legal judgment.

"The courts can't clamp information any more," Abdul says. "Judge Kovacs stopped the mainstream press, but we aren't the mainstream press – we are the new media."

COVER STORY – SIDEBAR 1

UNIVERSITIES AND POLICE

by K.K. CAMPBELL

University of Western Ontario's computer security officer Reg Quinton told *eye* he isn't interested in discussing whether the Homolka FAQ is legal or not – if the police say it's illegal, that's good enough for him.

But Ontario authorities, from the attorney-general on down, are painfully confused about how Karla, the ban and the Internet relate. Yet here we have Western's security officer saying quite bluntly he doesn't care. He will cooperate with police for fear his computers will be confiscated if he doesn't.

Quinton's open letter of March 28 addresses Western students: "If you think the University is going to protect your 'right' to break the law, you are sadly mistaken. The law applies here just as much as elsewhere.

You don't have a right to violate the publication ban – don't expect any sympathy or support if you do."

Since no one knows how the law applies, Quinton's actually saying: "If you think the University is going to protect you against the police, regardless if they are right or wrong, you are sadly mistaken."

Carl M. Kadie (kadie@hal.cs.uiuc.edu), founder of the Internet's Computers and Academic Freedom newsletter, thinks Quinton's position is dangerous – though he understands university computer staff confusion.

Computer administrators have no history of standing up to the police or the state. Librarians, on the other hand, have decades of precedent in demanding subpoenas and warrants when authority comes calling. Computer administrators lack this training and tradition.

Karen Adams, executive director of the Canadian Library Association, told *eye* a librarian would probably have demanded a warrant before revealing if Lt Starbuck even had an account at a library.

Kadie says that computer administrators desperately need to develop similar ethics. "Just as a professional librarian would have been less likely than the computer system administrators to turn over personal information to the police, so professional reporters are less likely than students under the gun to disclose sources to the authorities," Kadie told *eye*.

"The promise of the information superhighway is that we all become librarians and reporters. The danger right now is most people don't understand the responsibilities that come with their new roles."

Reprinted with the kind permission of the author.

The original text is available through anonymous ftp from eye.org in the directory /pub/eye.WEEKLY/back.issues/05.19, or from eye WEEKLY, 57 Spadina Avenue, Suite 207, Toronto, Ontario, Canada M5V 2J2.

Appendix D

The Institution of Analysts and Programmers

Although they currently have no formally approved ethical code, the UK-based Institution of Analysts and Programmers does have views on ethical issues, and is developing firmer procedures. Asked for information on their policies, the Director General of the Institute contributed this statement, which is reproduced with his permission.

The Institution and Ethics

The Institution of Analysts and Programmers is Britain's leading specialised professional body for those who work in these particular fields. One of the Institution's principal aims is to promote high standards of professional and ethical conduct amongst its members.

More than ten years ago the Institution pioneered a model Data Process Contract. A substantial number of IAP members are independent software producers, and the model contract was intended principally to provide those members with a basic commercial tool. In fact its clauses addressed a number of areas that were more ethical than commercial, and it thus provided the first formal definition of the Institution's position on ethical matters.

Ten years on the world is a much harder place for software producers. Not only is there more commercial competition, but customers are harder to satisfy because consumer legislation has made them more aware of their rights. In the old days the IT industry spread the myth that computers could work miracles: now we are reaping the consequences. Clients are finding out what we knew all along – that computers cannot solve complicated problems unless they are fed equally complicated instructions. Writing these instructions is a slow and costly process, and mistakes are easily made.

The Institution decided that in today's climate members would welcome a firmer lead in ethical and professional matters. A committee of the Council has been set up, and a report is expected in a few months' time. The issue is being looked at from two opposing directions: from the viewpoint of IAP members, and from the viewpoint of clients and members of the public.

At one level it is hoped to establish simple guidelines for the drafting of contracts, and for the behaviour of the parties involved. But eventually we would like to back this with some much more comprehensive instruction on commercial matters generally, covering those areas most affecting our members, and where some of them are sadly ignorant. Increasing numbers of professional people are working as independent consultants: this is a trend particularly affecting IT. Many of our members who trained as programmers now find themselves struggling to be salesmen, lawyers and accountants as well! Some of them are not very good at it, and perhaps the Institution should try to help them.

One of the advantages of having clearly defined rules for the conduct for IAP members is that it makes it easier to determine the point at which a member's conduct becomes unacceptable. The final part of our current review will establish sanctions to be applied to persons whose conduct might bring the Institution itself into disrepute if they are allowed to remain as members.

MICHAEL C. RYAN

Director General
The Institution of Analysts & Programmers
12th September 1994

The Institution of Analysts & Programmers
Charles House, 36 Culmington Road, London W13 9NH
0181-576-2118

Appendix E

BCS and ACM codes of conduct

This appendix contains the text of the British Computer Society's Code of Conduct and the official summary of the Code of Ethics and Professional Conduct of the Association for Computing Machinery, both of which are discussed in Chapter 7.

The Codes are reproduced with the kind permission of the BCS and ACM.

British Computer Society Code of Conduct

Rules of Professional Conduct

As an aid to understanding, these rules have been grouped in the principal duties which all members should endeavour to discharge in pursuing their professional lives.

The Public Interest

1. Members shall in their professional practice safeguard public health and safety and have regard to the protection of the environment.
2. Members shall have due regard to the legitimate rights of third parties.
3. Members shall ensure that within their chosen fields they have knowledge and understanding of relevant legislation, regulations and standards and that they comply with such requirements.
4. Members shall in their professional practice have regard to basic human rights and shall avoid any actions that adversely affect such rights.

Duty to Employers and Clients

5. Members shall carry out work with due care and diligence in accordance with the requirements of the employer or client and shall, if their professional judgement is overruled, indicate the likely consequences.
6. Members shall endeavour to complete work undertaken on time and to budget and shall advise their employer or client as soon as practicable if any overrun is foreseen.
7. Members shall not offer or provide, or receive in return, any inducement for the introduction of business from a client unless there is full prior disclosure of the facts to that client.
8. Members shall not disclose or authorise to be disclosed, or use for personal gain or to benefit a third party, confidential information acquired in the course of professional practice, except with prior written permission of the employer or client or at the direction of a court of law.
9. Members should seek to avoid being put in a position where they may become privy to or party to activities or information concerning activities which would conflict with their responsibilities in 1–4 above.
10. Members should not misrepresent or withhold information on the capabilities of products, systems or services with which they are concerned or take advantage of the lack of knowledge or inexperience of others.
11. Members shall not, except where specifically so instructed, handle clients' monies or place contracts or orders in connection with work on which they knowingly have any interest, financial or otherwise.
12. Members shall not purport to exercise independent judgement on behalf of a client on any product or service which they knowingly have any interest, financial or otherwise.

Duty to the Profession

13. Members shall uphold the reputation of the Profession and shall seek to improve professional standards through participation in their development, use and enforcement, and shall avoid any action which will adversely affect the good standing of the Profession.

14. Members shall in their professional practice seek to advance public knowledge and understanding of computing and information systems and technology and to counter false or misleading statements which are detrimental to the Profession.

15. Members shall encourage and support fellow members in their professional development and, where possible, provide opportunities for the professional development of new entrants to the Profession.

16. Members shall act with integrity towards fellow members and to members of other professions with whom they are concerned in a professional capacity and shall avoid engaging in any activity which is incompatible with professional status.

17. Members shall not make any public statement in their professional capacity unless properly qualified and, where appropriate, authorised to do so, and shall have due regard to the likely consequences of any such statement on others.

Professional Competence and Integrity

18. Members shall seek to upgrade their professional knowledge and skill and shall maintain awareness of technological developments, procedures and standards which are relevant to their field, and shall encourage their subordinates to do likewise.

19. Members shall seek to conform to recognised good practice including quality standards which are in their judgement relevant, and shall encourage their subordinates to do likewise.

20. Members shall only offer to do work or provide service which is within their professional competence and shall not lay claim to any level of competence which they do not possess, and any professional opinion which they are asked to give shall be objective and reliable.

21. Members shall accept professional responsibility for their work and for the work of subordinates and associates under their direction, and shall not terminate any assignment except for good reason and on reasonable notice.

22. Members shall avoid any situation that may give rise to a conflict of interest between themselves and their client and shall make full and immediate disclosure to the client if any such conflict should occur.

ACM (Association for Computing Machinery)

Code of Ethics and Professional Conduct – Summary

Adopted by the ACM Council on 16 Oct 1992.

1. **General Moral Imperatives.**
    As an ACM member I will
    1.1 Contribute to society and human well-being
    1.2 Avoid harm to others
    1.3 Be honest and trustworthy
    1.4 Be fair and take action not to discriminate
    1.5 Honor property rights including copyrights and patents
    1.6 Give proper credit for intellectual property
    1.7 Respect the privacy of others
    1.8 Honor confidentiality

2. **More Specific Professional Responsibilities.**
    As an ACM computing professional, I will
    2.1 Strive to achieve the highest quality, effectiveness, and dignity in both the process and products of professional work.
    2.2 Acquire and maintain professional competence.
    2.3 Know and respect existing laws pertaining to professional work.
    2.4 Accept and provide appropriate professional review.
    2.5 Give comprehensive and thorough evaluations of computer systems and their impacts, including analysis of possible risks.
    2.6 Honor contracts, agreements, and assigned responsibilities.
    2.7 Improve public understanding of computing and its consequences.
    2.8 Access computing and communication resources only when authorized to do so.

3. **Organizational Leadership Imperatives.**

As an ACM member and an organizational leader, I will

3.1   Articulate social responsibilities of members of an organizational unit and encourage full acceptance of those responsibilities.

3.2   Manage personnel and resources to design and build information systems that enhance the quality of working life.

3.3   Acknowledge and support proper and authorized uses of an organization's computing and communication resources.

3.4   Ensure that users and those who will be affected by a system have their needs clearly articulated during the assessment and design of requirements; later, the system must be validated to meet [its] requirements.

3.5   Articulate and support policies that protect the dignity of users and others affected by a computing system.

3.6   Create opportunities for members of the organization to learn the principles and limitations of computer systems.

4. **Compliance With The Code.**

As an ACM member, I will

4.1   Uphold and promote the principles of this code.

4.2   Treat violations of this code as inconsistent with membership in the ACM.

Bibliography

This list is far from exhaustive, but all the books and articles listed here have been selected as potentially of interest to a student of computer ethics. They are grouped under appropriate headings.

Computer ethics

Two journal articles which may be useful :

Using the new ACM code of ethics in decision making, Anderson, R. E., Johnson, D. G., Gotterbarn, D. and Perrolle, J., *Communications of the ACM*, **36**, (1), February 1993, p. 98.

How good is good enough? An ethical analysis of software construction and use, Collins, W. R., Miller, K. W., Spielman, B. J. and Wherry, P., *Communications of the ACM*, **37**, (1), January 1994, p. 81.

Of available books, I would suggest :

Ethical Conflicts in Information and Computer Science, Technology and Business, Parker, D. B., Swope, S. and Baker, B. N., QED Inc., Wellesley, MA, 1990.

Ethical Issues in the Use of Computers, Johnson, D. G. and Snapper, J. W. (eds.), Wadsworth Publishing, Belmont, CA, 1985.

Computers, Ethics and Society, Ermann, M. D., Williams, M. B. and Gutierrez, C. (eds.), Oxford University Press, New York, 1990

Teaching Computer Ethics, Bynum, T., Maner, W. and Fodor, J. L. (eds.), Southern Connecticut State University, Research Center on Computing and Society, New Haven, CT, 1991.

Computerization and Controversy: Value Conflicts and Social Choices, Kling, R. (ed.), Academic Press, London, 1995.

Professional Awareness in Software Engineering, Myers, C. (ed.), McGraw-Hill, London, 1995.

Computer Ethics, Johnson, D. G., Prentice-Hall, London, 1985.

Computer Ethics: Cautionary Tales and Ethical Dilemmas in Computing, Forester, T. and Morrison, P., Basil Blackwell, Oxford, 1990.

Zen and the Art of Motorcycle Maintenance, Pirsig, R. M., Vintage Press, London, 1974.

The Cuckoo's Egg: Tracking a Spy Through the Maze of Computer Espionage, Stoll, C., Pan Books, London, 1991.

Hackers – Heroes of the Computer Revolution, Levy, S., Anchor Press/ Doubleday, New York, 1984.

Data protection

Data Protection: Putting the Record Straight, Cornwell, R. and Staunton, M., NCCL, London, 1985.

A Guide to the Data Protection Act, Savage, N. and Edwards, C., Financial Training Publications, London, 1985.

Not a book, but a relevant address:
The Data Protection Registry
Office of The Data Protection Registrar, Springfield House, Water Lane, Wilmslow, Cheshire SK9 5AX.

Enquiries	Wilmslow (01625) 535777
Administration	Wilmslow (01625) 535711
Fax	Wilmslow (01625) 524510

Computer law

Computer Law, Reed, C. (ed.), Blackstone Press, London, 1993.

Introduction to Computer Law, Bainbridge, D., Pitman, London, 1993.

Yearbook of Law, Computers and Technology, Arnold, C. (ed.), Butterworth, London (annually).

The Legal Aspects of Computing, Knight, P. and Fitzsimons, J., Addison-Wesley, Wokingham, 1990.

Ethics

Ethics: Inventing Right and Wrong, Mackie, J. L., Penguin, London, 1990.

Applied Ethics, Singer, P. (ed.), Oxford University Press, Oxford, 1986.

Ethics, Singer, P. (ed.), Oxford University Press, Oxford, 1994.

Ethics in the History of Western Philosophy, Cavalier, R. J., Gouinlock, J. and Sterba, J. P. (eds.), Macmillan, Basingstoke, 1989.